I0412004

READINGS IN LENINISM
No. 3

THE DICTATORSHIP
OF THE PROLETARIAT

First Published in the United States, 1936

Republished by Red Star Publishers, 2014
www.RedStarPublishers.org

NOTE

This volume is one of a series of "Readings in Leninism." Each book consists of a collection of articles and extracts – taken almost exclusively from the works of Marx, Engels, Lenin and Stalin – dealing with a basic question of Leninist theory.

The key passages included in these volumes are not designed to serve as a substitute for reading the fundamental works of Marxism-Leninism in their entirety. The purpose of the series is to assemble, within the covers of a single book, pertinent excerpts dealing with a specific problem of primary importance, such as the theory of the proletarian revolution, the dictatorship of the proletariat, strategy and tactics of the proletarian revolution, the national and agrarian questions, etc.

Systematically compiled and arranged by V. Bystryansky and M. Mishin, this material should be extremely helpful as a guide to individual or group study of the fundamental principles of Leninism.

The present volume is concerned with the Marxist-Leninist doctrine of the state; the dictatorship of the proletariat and its three main aspects; the Soviets as a state form of the proletarian dictatorship; the strengthening of the state power of the proletariat and the conditions for the withering away of the state.

CONTENTS

I. THE MARXIST-LENINIST DOCTRINE OF THE STATE

1. The Essence of the State as a Dictatorship Set Up by One Class Over the Other

A. The State as the Product of the Irreconcilability of the Class Contradictions

What is now happening to Marx's doctrine has, in the course of history, often happened to the doctrines of other revolutionary thinkers and leaders of oppressed classes struggling for emancipation. During the lifetime of great revolutionaries, the oppressing classes relentlessly persecute them and meet their teachings with the most savage hostility, the most furious hatred and the most ruthless campaign of lies and slanders. After their death, attempts are made to convert them into harmless icons, to canonize them, so to say, and to surround their *names* with a certain halo for the "consolation" of the oppressed classes and with the object of duping them. At the same time the *content* of their revolutionary doctrine is emasculated and vulgarized and its revolutionary edge is blunted. At the present time, the bourgeoisie and the opportunists in the labor movement are cooperating in this work of "revising" Marxism. They omit, obliterate, and distort the revolutionary side of its doctrine, its revolutionary soul. They push to the foreground and extol what is, or seems, acceptable to the bourgeoisie. All the social-chauvinists are now "Marxists" (don't laugh!). And more and more frequently, German bourgeois professors, erstwhile specialists in the extermination of Marxism, are speaking of the "national-German" Marx, who, they aver, trained the labor unions which are so splendidly organized for the purpose of conducting a predatory war!

In such circumstances, in view of the incredibly widespread nature of the distortions of Marxism, our first task is to *restore* the true doctrine of Marx on the state. For this purpose it will be necessary to quote at length from the works of Marx and Engels. Of course, long quotations will make the text cumbersome and will not help to make it popular reading, but we cannot possibly avoid them. All, or at any rate, all the most essential passages in the works of Marx and Engels on the subject of the state must necessarily be given as fully as possible, in order that the reader may form an independent opinion on all the views of the founders of scientific Socialism and on the development of those views, and in order that their distortion by the now prevailing "Kautskyism" may be documentarily proved and clearly demonstrated.

Let us begin with the most popular of Engels' works, *Der Ursprung der Familie, das Privateigentums und des Staats*[*] the sixth edition of which was published in Stuttgart as far back as 1894....

Summing up his historical analysis, Engels says:

> The state is therefore by no means a power imposed on society from the outside; just as little is it "the reality of the moral idea," "the image and reality of reason," as Hegel asserts. Rather, it is a product of society at a certain stage of development; it is the admission that this society has become entangled in an insoluble contradiction with itself, that it is cleft into irreconcilable antagonisms, which it is powerless to dispel. But in order that these antagonisms, classes with conflicting economic interests, might not consume themselves and society in sterile struggle, a power apparently standing above society became necessary, for the purpose of moderating the conflict and keeping it within the bounds of "order"; and this power, arising out of society, but placing itself above it, and increasingly alienating itself from it, is the state.

This fully expresses the basic idea of Marxism on the question of the historical role and meaning of the state. The state is the product and the manifestation of the *irreconcilability* of class antagonisms. The state arises when, where, and to the extent that the class antagonisms *cannot* be objectively reconciled. And, conversely, the existence of the state proves that the class antagonisms *are* irreconcilable.

It is precisely on this most important and fundamental point that distortions of Marxism, proceeding along two main lines, begin.

On the one hand, the bourgeois ideologists, and particularly the petty-bourgeois ideologists, compelled by the pressure of indisputable historical facts to admit that the state only exists where there are class antagonisms and the class struggle, "correct" Marx in a way that makes it appear that the state is an organ for the conciliation of classes. According to Marx, the state could neither arise nor contin-

---

[*] Frederick Engels, *The Origin of the Family, Private Property, and the State. – Ed.*

ue to exist if it were possible to conciliate classes. According to the petty-bourgeois and philistine professors and publicists – frequently on the strength of benevolent references to Marx! – the state conciliates classes. According to Marx, the state is an organ of class *rule,* an organ for the *oppression* of one class by another; it creates "order" which legalizes and perpetuates this oppression by moderating the collisions between the classes. In the opinion of the petty-bourgeois politicians, order means the conciliation of classes, and not the oppression of one class by another; to moderate collisions means to conciliate and not deprive the oppressed classes of definite means and methods of fighting to overthrow the oppressors.

For instance, when, in the Revolution of 1917, the question of the real meaning and role of the state arose in all its grandeur, as a practical question demanding immediate action on a wide mass scale, all the Socialist-Revolutionaries and Mensheviks immediately and completely sank to the petty-bourgeois theory that the "state" "conciliates" classes. Innumerable resolutions and articles by politicians of both these parties are thoroughly saturated with this purely petty-bourgeois and philistine "conciliation" theory. Petty-bourgeois democracy is never able to understand that the state is the organ of the rule of a definite class which *cannot* be reconciled with its antipode (the class opposed to it). Their attitude towards the state is one of the most striking proofs that our Socialist-Revolutionaries and Mensheviks are not Socialists at all (which we Bolsheviks have always maintained), but petty-bourgeois democrats with near-Socialist phraseology.

On the other hand, the "Kautskyan" distortion of Marx is far more subtle. "Theoretically," it is not denied that the state is the organ of class rule, or that class antagonisms are irreconcilable. But what is forgotten or glossed over is this: If the state is the product of irreconcilable class antagonisms, if it is a power standing *above* society and *"increasingly alienating itself from it,"* it is clear that the liberation of the oppressed class is impossible, not only without a violent revolution, *but also without the destruction* of the apparatus of state power which was created by the ruling class and which is the embodiment of this "alienation." As we shall see later, Marx very definitely drew this theoretically self-evident conclusion from a concrete historical analysis of the tasks of the revolution. And – as we shall show fully in our subsequent remarks – it is precisely this conclusion which Kautsky has "forgotten" and distorted.

B. The Military Bureaucratic Apparatus of the Bourgeois State

Engels continues:

> As against the ancient *gentile* organization, the primary distinguishing feature of the state is the division of the subjects of the state *according to* territory.[*]

Such a division seems "natural" to us, but it cost a prolonged struggle against the old form of tribal or gentile society.

> ...The second is the establishment of a *public power,* which is no longer directly identical with the population organizing itself as an armed power. This special public power is necessary, because a self-acting armed organization of the population has become impossible since the cleavage of society into classes.... This public power exists in every state; it consists not merely of armed men, but of material appendages, prisons and coercive institutions of all kinds, of which gentile society knew nothing....[†]

Engels further elucidates the concept of the "power" which is termed the state – a power which arises from society, but which places itself above it and becomes more and more alienated from it. What does this power mainly consist of? It consists of special bodies of armed men which have prisons, etc., at their disposal.

We are justified in speaking of special bodies of armed men, because the public power which is an attribute of every state is not "directly identical" with the armed population, with its "self-acting armed organization."

Like all the great revolutionary thinkers, Engels tried to draw the attention of the class conscious workers to the very fact which prevailing philistinism regards as least worthy of attention, as the most common and sanctified, not only by long standing, but, one might say, petrified prejudices. A standing army and police are the chief instruments of state power. But can it be otherwise?

From the point of view of the vast majority of Europeans of the end of the nineteenth century whom Engels was addressing and who have not lived through or closely observed a single great revolution,

---

[*] *Ibid.*

[†] *Ibid.*

it cannot be otherwise. They completely fail to understand what a "self-acting armed organization of the population" is. To the question, whence arose the need for special bodies of armed men, standing above society and becoming alienated from it (police and standing army), the Western European and Russian philistines are inclined to answer with a few phrases borrowed from Spencer or Mikhailovsky, by referring to the complexity of social life, the differentiation of functions, and so forth.

Such a reference seems "scientific"; it effectively dulls the senses of the average man and obscures the most important and basic fact, namely, the cleavage of society into irreconcilably antagonistic classes. Had this cleavage not existed, the "self-acting armed organization of the population" might have differed from the primitive organization of a tribe of monkeys grasping sticks, or of primitive man, or of men united in a tribal form of society, by its complexity, its high technique, and so forth; but it would still have been possible.

It is impossible now, because civilized society is divided into antagonistic and, indeed, irreconcilably antagonistic classes, the "self-acting" arming of which would lead to an armed struggle between them. A state arises, a special force is created in the form of special bodies of armed men, and every revolution, by destroying the state apparatus, demonstrates to us how the ruling class strives to restore the special bodies of armed men which serve *it,* and how the oppressed class strives to create a new organization of this kind, capable of serving not the exploiters but the exploited.

In the above argument, Engels raises theoretically the very question which every great revolution raises practically, palpably and on a mass scale of action, namely, the question of the relation between special bodies of armed men and the "self-acting armed organization of the population." We shall see how this is concretely illustrated by the experience of the European and Russian revolutions.

But let us return to Engels' exposition.

He points out that sometimes, in certain parts of North America, for example, this public power is weak (he has in mind a rare exception in capitalist society, and he speaks about parts of North America in its pre-imperialist days, where the free colonist predominated), but that in general it tends to become stronger.

> It [the public power] grows stronger, however, in proportion as the class antagonisms within the state become

more acute, and with the growth in size and population of the adjacent states. We have only to look at our present-day Europe, where class struggle and rivalry in conquest have screwed up the public power to such a pitch that it threatens to devour the whole of society and even the state itself.[*]

This was written as early as the beginning of the 'nineties of the last century, Engels' last preface being dated June 16, 1891. The turn towards imperialism – meaning by that the complete domination of the trusts, the omnipotence of the big banks, and a colonial policy on a grand scale, and so forth – was only just beginning in France, and was even weaker in North America and in Germany. Since then "rivalry in conquest" has made gigantic progress – especially as, by the beginning of the second decade of the twentieth century, the whole world had been finally divided up among these "rivals in conquest," *i.e.,* among the great predatory powers. Since then, military and naval armaments have grown to monstrous proportions, and the predatory war of 1914-17 for the domination of the world by England or Germany, for the division of the spoils, has brought the "devouring" of all the forces of society by the rapacious state power to the verge of complete catastrophe.

As early as 1891, Engels was able to point to "rivalry in conquest" as one of the most important distinguishing features of the foreign policy of the Great Powers, but in 1914-17, when this rivalry, many times intensified, has given birth to an imperialist war, the rascally social-chauvinists cover up their defense of the predatory interests of "their" bourgeoisie by phrases about "defense of the fatherland," "defense of the republic and the revolution," etc.!

C. *The State as an Instrument for the Exploitation of the Oppressed Class*

For the maintenance of a special public power standing above society, taxes and state loans are needed.

> ...Possessing the public power and the right to exact taxes, the officials now exist as organs of society standing *above* society. The free, voluntary respect which was accorded to the organs of the gentile organization does not

---

[*] *Ibid.*

satisfy them, even if they could have it.*

Special laws proclaiming the sanctity and the immunity of the officials are enacted. "The shabbiest police servant" has more "authority" than all the representatives of the tribe put together, and even the head of the military power of a civilized state may well envy a tribal chief the "unfeigned and undisputed respect" the latter enjoys.

Here the question of the privileged position of the officials as organs of state power is stated. The main point indicated is: What puts them *above* society? We shall see how this theoretical problem was solved in practice by the Paris Commune in 1871 and how it was slurred over in a reactionary manner by Kautsky in 1912.

> As the state arose out of the need to hold class antagonisms in check, but as, at the same time, it arose in the midst of the conflict of these classes, it is, as a rule, the state of the most powerful, economically dominant class, which, through the medium of the state, becomes also the dominant class politically, and thus acquires new means of holding down and exploiting the oppressed class....†

It was not only the ancient and feudal states that were organs for the exploitation of the slaves and serfs, but

> ...the contemporary representative state is an instrument of exploitation of wage labor by capital. By way of exception, however, periods occur when the warring classes are so nearly balanced that the state power, ostensibly appearing as a mediator, acquires, for the moment, a certain independence in relation to both...‡

Such, for instance, were the absolute monarchies of the seventeenth and eighteenth centuries, the Bonapartism of the First and Second Empires in France, and the Bismarck regime in Germany. Such, we add, is the present Kerensky government in republican Russia since it began to persecute the revolutionary proletariat, at the moment when, thanks to the leadership of the petty-bourgeois

---

* *Ibid.*

† *Ibid.*

‡ *Ibid.*

democrats, the Soviets have *already* become impotent, while the bourgeoisie is *not yet* strong enough openly to disperse them.

In a democratic republic, Engels continues, "wealth wields its power indirectly, but all the more effectively," first, by means of the "direct corruption of the officials" (America); second, by means of "the alliance between the government and the Stock Exchange" (France and America).

At the present time, imperialism and the domination of the banks have "developed" both these methods of defending and asserting the omnipotence of wealth in democratic republics of all descriptions to an unusually fine art. For instance, in the very first months of the Russian democratic republic, one might say during the honeymoon of the union of the "Socialists" – Socialist-Revolutionaries and Mensheviks – with the bourgeoisie, Mr. Palchinsky, in the coalition government, obstructed every measure intended for the purpose of restraining the capitalists and their marauding practices, their plundering of the public treasury by means of war contracts. When Mr. Palchinsky resigned (replaced, of course, by an exactly similar Palchinsky) the capitalists "rewarded" him with a "soft" job and a salary of 120,000 rubles per annum. What would you call this – direct or indirect corruption? An alliance between the government and the syndicates, or "only" friendly relations? What role do the Chernovs, Tseretelis, Avksentyevs and Skobelevs play? Are they the "direct" or only the indirect allies of the millionaire treasury looters?

The omnipotence of "wealth" is thus more *secure* in a democratic republic, since it does not depend on the faulty political shell of capitalism. A democratic republic is the best possible political shell for capitalism, and therefore, once capital has gained control of this very best shell (through the Palchinskys, Chernovs, Tseretelis and Co.) it establishes its power so securely, so firmly, that *no* change, either of persons, of institutions, or of parties in the bourgeois democratic republic can shake it.

We must also note that Engels very definitely calls universal suffrage a means of bourgeois rule. Universal suffrage, he says, obviously summing up the long experience of German Social-Democracy, is an index of the maturity of the working class. It cannot and never will be anything more in the present state.

The petty-bourgeois democrats, such as our Socialist-Revolutionaries and Mensheviks, and also their twin brothers, the social-chauvinists and opportunists of Western Europe, all expect "more" from universal suffrage. They themselves adhere to, and instill into the minds of the people, the wrong idea that universal suffrage "in the *modern* state" is really capable of expressing the will of the majority of the toilers and of insuring its realization.

Here we can only note this wrong idea, only point out that Engels' perfectly clear, precise, and concrete statement is distorted at every step in the propaganda and agitation conducted by the "official" (*i.e.*, opportunist) Socialist parties. A detailed elucidation of the utter falsity of this idea, which Engels brushes aside, is given in our further account of the views of Marx and Engels on the *"modern"* state.

Engels gives a general summary of his views in the most popular of his works in the following words:

> The state, therefore, has not existed from all eternity. There have been societies which managed without it, which had no conception of the state and state power. At a certain stage of economic development, which was necessarily bound up with the cleavage of society into classes, the state became a necessity owing to this cleavage. We are now rapidly approaching a stage in the development of production at which the existence of these classes has not only ceased to be a necessity, but is becoming a positive hindrance to production. They will fall as inevitably as they arose at an earlier stage. Along with them, the state will inevitably fall. The society that organizes production anew on the basis of the free and equal association of the producers will put the whole state machine where it will then belong: in the museum of antiquities, side by side with the spinning wheel and the bronze ax.[*]

We do not often come across this passage in the propaganda and agitation literature of present-day Social-Democracy. But even when we do come across it, it is generally quoted in the same manner as one bows before an icon, *i.e.,* it is done merely to show official respect for Engels, and no attempt is made to gauge the breadth and depth of the revolution presupposed by this relegating of "the whole state machine... to the museum of antiquities." In most cases

---

[*] *Ibid.*

we do not even find an understanding of what Engels calls the state machine.

V. I. Lenin, *The State and Revolution,* London and New York, 1932, pp. 7-15.

2. The Breaking Up of the Bourgeois State Machine is a Necessary Condition of the Proletarian Revolution

It is well known that in the autumn of 1870, a few months before the Commune, Marx warned the Paris workers that an attempt to overthrow the government would be desperate folly. But when, in March 1871, a decisive battle was *forced* upon the workers and they accepted it, when the uprising had become a fact, Marx greeted the proletarian revolution with the greatest enthusiasm, in spite of unfavorable auguries. Marx did not assume the rigid attitude of pedantically condemning a "premature" movement as did the ill-famed Russian renegade from Marxism, Plekhanov, who, in November 1905, wrote encouragingly about the workers' and peasants' struggle but, after December 1905, cried, liberal fashion: "They should not have taken to arms."

Marx, however, was not only enthusiastic about the heroism of the Communards who "stormed the heavens" as he expressed it. Although it did not achieve its aim, he regarded the mass revolutionary movement as an historic experiment of gigantic importance, as an advance of the world proletarian revolution, as a practical step that was more important than hundreds of programs and discussions. Marx conceived his task to be to analyze this experiment, to draw lessons in tactics from it, to reexamine his theory in the new light it afforded.

Marx made the only "correction" he thought it necessary to make in *The Communist Manifesto* on the basis of the revolutionary experience of the Paris Communards.

The last preface to the new German edition of *The Communist Manifesto* signed by both its authors is dated June 24, 1872. In this preface the authors, Karl Marx and Frederick Engels, say that the program of *The Communist Manifesto* is now "in places out of date," and they go on to say:

> *One thing especially was proved by the Commune, viz.,* that the "working class cannot simply lay hold of the ready-made state machine and wield it for its own purposes."

The authors took the words in quotation marks in the above-quoted passage from Marx's book, *The Civil War in France.*

Thus, Marx and Engels regarded one of the principal and fundamental lessons of the Paris Commune as being of such enormous importance that they introduced it as a vital correction in *The Communist Manifesto.*

It is extremely characteristic that it is precisely this vital correction that has been distorted by the opportunists, and its meaning, probably, is not known to nine-tenths, if not ninety-nine-hundredths, of the readers of *The Communist Manifesto.* We shall deal with this distortion more fully further on, in a chapter devoted specially to distortions. Here it will be sufficient to note that the current vulgar "interpretation" of Marx's famous utterance quoted above is that Marx here emphasizes the idea of gradual development in contradistinction to the seizure of power, and so on.

As a matter of fact, *exactly the opposite is the case.* Marx's idea is that the working class must *break up, smash* the "ready-made state machine," and not confine itself merely to laying hold of it.

On April 12, 1871, *i.e.,* just at the time of the Commune, Marx wrote to Kugelmann:

> If you look at the last chapter of my *Eighteenth Brumaire,* you will see that I say that the next attempt of the French Revolution will be no longer, as before, to transfer the bureaucratic military machine from one hand to the other, but to *smash* [Marx's italics – the original is *zerbrechen*]; and this is essential for every real people's revolution on the Continent. And this is what our heroic Party comrades in Paris are attempting.[*]

The words, "to smash" "the bureaucratic military state machine," briefly express the principal lesson of Marxism on the task of the proletariat in relation to the state during a revolution. And it is precisely this lesson that has been not only forgotten, but positively distorted, in the prevailing Kautskyan "interpretation" of Marxism.

V. I. Lenin, *The State and Revolution,* pp. 32-34.

---

[*] *Editor's note:* The question of the possibility for the proletariat to win power without smashing the bourgeois state machine in England and America in the 'seventies is dealt with on pp. 63-64.

3. The Fight Against Anarchism and Bukharin's Semi-Anarchist Errors on the Question of the State

Allow me to recall the well-known theoretical dispute between Lenin and Bukharin on the question of the state, which developed in 1916. That is important in order to reveal both the inordinate claims of Comrade Bukharin to teach Lenin, and the roots of his theoretical unsoundness on such important questions as the dictatorship of the proletariat, the class struggle, etc. As you know, in 1916, an article by Comrade Bukharin appeared in the magazine *Youth International,* signed *Nota Bene,* which, as a matter of fact, was directed against Comrade Lenin. In his article Comrade Bukharin writes:

> ...It is absolutely wrong to seek the differences between the Socialists and the Anarchists in the fact that the former are advocates and the latter opponents of the state. As a matter of fact, the real difference between them is that revolutionary Social-Democracy wants to organize social production on new, centralized lines, *i.e.,* technically the most progressive, whereas decentralized anarchist production would mean a step backward to the old technique, to the old form of enterprise....

> ...Social-Democracy, which is, or which, at any rate, should be the teacher of the masses, now more than ever must emphasize its hostility in principle to the state. The present war has shown how deeply the roots of the state have penetrated the soul of the workers.

Comrade Lenin replied in a special article, criticizing the views of Comrade Bukharin, published in 1916. He said:

> That is wrong. The author raises the question as to what is the difference between the attitude of the Socialists and the Anarchists towards the state, but he replies not to *this question,* but to *another,* namely, what is the difference in their attitude towards the economic basis of the future of society? That, of course, is a very important and necessary question. But it does not follow from that that the *main point* of the difference in the attitude of the Socialists and Anarchists towards the state can be overlooked. Socialists are in favor of utilizing the modern state and its institutions in the struggle for the emancipation of the working class and are equally in

favor of utilizing the state for the peculiar form of transition from capitalism to socialism. This transitional form, which is *also* a state, is the dictatorship of the proletariat. The Anarchists want to "abolish" the state, to "blow it up" (*sprengen*), as Comrade *Nota Bene* expresses it in one place, erroneously attributing this view to the socialists. The socialists – unfortunately the author quotes the words of Engels relevant to this subject far too inadequately – recognize that the state will "gradually" die out, will "fall asleep" *after* the bourgeoisie has been expropriated....

...In order to "emphasize" "hostility" to the state "on principle," it is necessary to understand it "clearly," and it is just this clarity which the author lacks. The phrase regarding "the roots of the state" is absolutely muddled, non-Marxian, non-socialist. It is not that "state" has clashed with the negation of state, but that the opportunist policy (*i.e.*, an opportunist, reformist, bourgeois attitude to the state) has clashed with revolutionary Social-Democratic policy (*i.e.*, the revolutionary Social-Democratic attitude to the bourgeois state and towards the utilization of the state against the bourgeoisie in order to overthrow it). These are absolutely and entirely different things. (V. I. Lenin, *Collected Works*, Russian edition, Vol. XIX, p. 296.)

I think the point of issue is clear, and I think the semi-anarchistic mess Comrade Bukharin has got himself into is also clear.

Sten: At that time Lenin had not yet fully formulated the necessity for "blowing up" the state. Bukharin, while committing anarchist errors, was approaching a formulation of the question.

Stalin: No, Comrade Sten, that is not the point at present. The point is the attitude toward the state in general. The 20 point is that, according to Comrade Bukharin, the working class should be hostile *in principle* to the *state as such,* including the working class state.

Sten: Lenin then only talked about utilizing the state; he said nothing in his criticism of Comrade Bukharin regarding the "blowing up" of the state.

Stalin: You are mistaken, Comrade Sten. Let me assure you that the point here is that, in the opinion of Comrade Bukharin (and of the Anarchists), the workers should emphasize their hostility in principle to the state as such, and, hence, to the state of the transition period, to the working class state. Try to explain to our workers that the working class must become imbued with hostility in principle to the proletarian dictatorship which, of course, is also a state. Comrade Bukharin's position as set forth in his article in *Youth International* is that he repudiates the state in the period of transition from capitalism to socialism. Comrade Bukharin here overlooked a "trifle," namely, the whole transition period, during which the working class cannot get along without its own state, if it really wants to crush the bourgeoisie and build socialism. That is the first point. The second point is that it is not true that Comrade Lenin at that time did not deal in his criticism with the theory of the "blowing up," or the "abolition" of the state in general. Lenin not only dealt with that theory, as is obvious from the passages I have cited, but he criticized it to bits, as an anarchist theory, and opposed it by the theory of the *creation* of a new state after the overthrow of the bourgeoisie, namely, the state of the proletarian dictatorship. Finally, the anarchist theory of "blowing up" the state must not be confused with the Marxist theory of the "breaking up," the "smashing" of the *bourgeois* state machine. Certain comrades are inclined to confuse these two distinct conceptions in the belief that they are an expression of one and the same idea. But that is wrong, comrades, absolutely wrong. Lenin proceeded only from the Marxist theory of the "smashing" of the bourgeois state machine when he criticized the anarchist theory of "blowing up" and "abolishing" the state in general.

Joseph Stalin, *Leninism,* Vol. II, pp. 145-147. From the minutes of the Plenum of the Central Committee, Communist Party of the Soviet Union, held in April 1929, at which this speech was delivered.

4. The Bourgeois State and Its Forms

A. Bourgeois Democracy – A Veiled Form of the Dictatorship of the Bourgeoisie

I have already mentioned to you Engels' work, *The Origin of the Family, Private Property and the State* as an aid. Here it is precisely stated that any state, however democratic, where private property exists in land and in the means of production and where capital predominates, is a capitalist state, a machinery in the hands of the capitalists for the purpose of holding in subjection the working class and the poor peasantry; whereas universal suffrage, the

Constituent Assembly and Parliament are merely a form, a kind of promissory note which essentially does not alter the case.

The forms of state domination may vary: capital manifests its force in one manner where there is one form and in a different manner where there is another, but in essence power remains in the hands of capital. Capital, once it exists, dominates society and no democratic republic, no electoral law alters this fact.

The democratic republic and universal suffrage marked an enormous progress as compared with serfdom: they offered the proletariat the possibility of achieving its present unity and consolidation, and of forming the serried disciplined ranks which wage a systematic fight against capitalism. The serf peasant, let alone the slaves, knew nothing that in any way resembled it. The slaves, as we know, many a time revolted, rioted, fought in civil wars, but at no time were they able to form a class conscious majority or create parties which would lead the fight; they were unable clearly to understand what they were aiming at and always, even in the most revolutionary periods of history, proved to be pawns in the hands of the ruling classes. The bourgeois republic, parliament, universal suffrage – all this represents tremendous progress from the point of view of the world development of society. Humanity progressed towards capitalism and only capitalism, thanks to urban culture, enabled the oppressed class of proletarians to find itself and create the world labor movement, the millions of workers all over the world who are organized into parties – the socialist parties which consciously lead the struggle of the masses. Without parliamentarism, without the suffrage this development of the working class would have proved impossible. That is why all this assumed such great importance in the eyes of the broad masses of the people. That is why the change appears so difficult. Not only deliberate hypocrites, scientists and clergymen, but also masses of people who innocently repeat the old prejudices and cannot understand the transition from old capitalist society to socialism, maintain and defend this bourgeois lie that the state is free and is called upon to defend the interests of all. Not only people who directly depend upon the bourgeoisie, not only those who are under the yoke of capital or those who are bribed by capital (a large number of various scientists, artists, clergymen and so on, are in the service of capital), but also people who are merely under the influence of the bourgeois freedom prejudices, have risen against Bolshevism all the world over because the Soviet Republic at its inception had discarded this bourgeois lie and openly declared: You call your state a free state but in fact, as long as private property exists, your state, even if it is a democratic republic, is nothing but an instrument in the hands of the capitalists for the oppression of the workers, and the freer the state the more clearly is it manifested....

...No matter what forms the republic, even the most democratic republic, assumes, if it is a bourgeois republic, if private property in land, mills and factories still obtains and private capital holds society in wage slavery, *i.e.,* if the declarations contained in the program of our Party and in the Soviet constitution are not being carried out in that republic, then this state is a machine for the oppression of some people by others. And we will get this machine into the hands of the class which must overthrow the rule of capital. We will discard all the old prejudices that the state means general equality – this is deceit: as long as exploitation exists there can be no equality. The landlord cannot be the worker's equal, the hungry man the equal of the well fed. The machine which is called the state, before which people stopped in superstitious awe, believing the old stories that it is the power of the whole people – that machine the proletariat discards, pronouncing it a bourgeois lie. We have taken that machine from the capitalists, taken it for ourselves. By means of this machine or club we will put an end to all exploitation and when all opportunities for exploitation disappear and there are no land or factory owners left in the world, there will be no such thing as some people gorging while others are starving – only then will we scrap this machine. Then there will be no state, no exploitation. This is the point of view of our Communist Party.

V. I. Lenin, *Collected Works,* Russian edition, Vol. XXIV, pp. 374-377.

B. "Fascism – the Open, Terrorist Dictatorship of the Most Reactionary, Most Chauvinist and Most Imperialist Elements of Finance Capital."

Now the time is approaching when, by force of objective reasons, this period of German history covering half a century *must* be followed by another period. The epoch during which the legality created by the bourgeoisie was made use of is *followed* by an epoch of great revolutionary battles, and these battles will *in essence* signify the demolition of the *entire* bourgeois legality, the *entire* bourgeois system, while at the beginning they must assume (and are assuming) *the form,* of confused attempts on the part of the bourgeoisie to get rid of the legality which it itself created but which has become intolerable for it. "Bourgeois gentlemen, you shoot first!" This phrase, written by Engels in 1894, expresses the peculiar situation and the peculiar tactical problems of the revolutionary proletariat.*

...The epoch of imperialism, the sharpening of the class struggle and the growth of the elements of civil war – particularly after the imperialist war – led to the bankruptcy of parliamentarism. Hence, the adoption of "new" methods and forms of administration (for example, the system of inner cabinets, the formation of oligarchical groups, acting behind the scenes, the deterioration and falsification of the function of "popular representation," the restriction and annulment of "democratic liberties," etc.). Under certain special historical conditions, the progress of this bourgeois imperialist, reactionary offensive assumes the form of Fascism. These conditions are: instability of capitalist relationships; the existence of considerable declassed social elements, the pauperization of broad strata of the urban petty bourgeoisie and of the intelligentsia; discontent among the rural petty bourgeoisie and, finally, the constant menace of mass proletarian action. In order to stabilize and perpetuate its rule, the bourgeoisie is compelled to an increasing degree to abandon the parliamentary system in favor of the Fascist system, which is independent of inter-party arrangements and combinations. The Fascist system is a system of direct dictatorship, ideologically marked by the "national idea" and representation of the "professions" (in reality, representation of the various groups of the ruling class). It is a system that resorts to a peculiar form of social demagogy (anti-Semitism, occasional sorties against usurers' capital and gestures of impatience with the parliamentary "talking shop") in order to utilize the discontent of the petty bourgeois, the intellectuals and other strata of society, and to corruption (the creation of a compact and well paid hierarchy of Fascist units, a party apparatus and a bureaucracy). At the same time, Fascism strives to permeate the working class by recruiting the most backward strata of workers to its ranks, by playing upon their discontent, by taking advantage

---

*V. I. Lenin, *Collected Works,* Russian edition, Vol. XIV, p. 381.

of the inaction of social democracy, etc. The principal aim of Fascism is to destroy the revolutionary labor vanguard, *i.e.,* the Communist sections and leading units of the proletariat. The combination of social demagogy, corruption and active white terror, in conjunction with extreme imperialist aggression in the sphere of foreign politics, are the characteristic features of Fascism. In periods of acute crisis for the bourgeoisie, Fascism resorts to anti-capitalist phraseology, but, after it has established itself at the helm of the state, it casts aside its anti-capitalist rattle and discloses itself as a terrorist dictatorship of big capital....

Program of the Communist International, Part II, Section 3.

As the Thirteenth Plenum of the Executive Committee of the Communist International correctly declared, fascism in power is *the open, terrorist dictatorship of the most reactionary, most chauvinist and most imperialist elements of finance capital.*

The most reactionary variety of fascism is *the German type* of fascism. It has the effrontery to call itself National-Socialism, though having nothing in common with Socialism. Hitler fascism is not only bourgeois nationalism, it is bestial chauvinism. It is a governmental system of political banditry, a system of provocation and torture practiced upon the working class and the revolutionary elements of the peasantry, the petty bourgeoisie and the intelligentsia. It is medieval barbarity and bestiality, it is unbridled aggression in relation to other nations and countries.

German fascism is acting as *the spearhead of international counter-revolution,* as *the chief incendiary of imperialist war, as the initiator of a crusade against the Soviet Union, the great fatherland of the toilers of the whole world.*

Fascism is not a form of state power "standing above both classes – the proletariat and the bourgeoisie," as Otto Bauer, for instance, has asserted. It is not "the revolt of the petty bourgeoisie which has captured the machinery of the state," as the British Socialist Brailsford declares. No, fascism is not super-class government, nor government of the petty bourgeoisie or the lumpen-proletariat over finance capital. Fascism is the power of finance capital itself. It is the organization of terrorist vengeance against the working class and the revolutionary section of the peasantry and intelligentsia. Fascism in foreign policy is chauvinism in its crudest form, fomenting the bestial hatred of other nations.

This, the true character of fascism, must be particularly stressed; because in a number of countries fascism, under cover of social demagogy, has managed to gain the following of the petty bourgeois masses who have been driven out of their course by the crisis, and even of certain sections of the most backward sections of the proletariat. These would never have supported fascism if they had understood its real class character and its true nature.

The development of fascism, and the fascist dictatorship itself, assume *different forms* in different countries, according to historical, social and economic conditions, and to the national peculiarities and the international position of the given country. In certain countries, principally those in which fascism does not enjoy a broad mass basis and in which the struggle of the various groups within the camp of the fascist bourgeoisie itself is fairly acute, fascism does not immediately venture to abolish parliament; it allows the other bourgeois parties, as well as the Social-Democratic Parties, to retain a certain degree of legality. In other countries, where the ruling bourgeoisie fears an *early* outbreak of revolution, fascism establishes its unrestricted political monopoly, either immediately or by intensifying its reign of terror against, and persecution of, all competing parties and groups. This does not prevent fascism, when its position becomes *particularly* acute, from endeavoring to extend its basis and without altering its class nature, *combining* open, terrorist dictatorship with a crude sham of parliamentarism.

The accession to power of fascism is not an *ordinary succession* of one bourgeois government by another, but a *substitution* for one state form of class domination of the bourgeois – bourgeois democracy – of another form – open, terrorist dictatorship. It would be a serious mistake to ignore this distinction, a mistake which would prevent the revolutionary proletariat from mobilizing the broadest sections of the toilers of town and country for the struggle against the menace of the seizure of power by the fascists, and from taking advantage of the contradictions which exist in the camp of the bourgeoisie itself. But it is a mistake no less serious and dangerous to *underrate* the importance, for the establishment of fascist dictatorship, of the *reactionary measures of the bourgeoisie which are at present being increasingly initiated in bourgeois-democratic countries* – measures which destroy the democratic liberties of the toilers, falsify and curtail the rights of parliament and intensify the repression of the revolutionary movement.

The accession to power of fascism must not be conceived of in so simplified and smooth a form, as though some committee or other of finance capital decided on a certain date to set up a fascist dictatorship. In reality, fascism usually comes to power in the course of a mutual, and at times severe, struggle against the old bourgeois parties, or a definite section of these parties, in the course of a struggle even within the fascist camp itself – a struggle which at times leads to armed clashes, as we have witnessed in the case of Germany, Austria and other countries. All this, however, does not detract from the fact that before the establishment of a fascist dictatorship, bourgeois governments usually pass through a number of preliminary stages and institute a number of reactionary measures, which directly facilitate the accession to power of fascism. Whoever does not fight the reactionary measures of the bourgeoisie and the growth of fascism at these preparatory stages *is not in a position to prevent the victory of fascism, but, on the contrary, facilitates that victory.*

The Social-Democratic leaders glossed over and concealed from the masses the true class nature of fascism, and did not call them to the struggle against the increasingly reactionary measures of the bourgeoisie. They bear great *historical responsibility* for the fact that at the decisive moment of the fascist offensive, a large section of the toiling masses of Germany and a number of other fascist countries failed to recognize in fascism the most bloodthirsty monster of finance, their most vicious enemy, and that these masses were not prepared to resist it.

What is the source of the influence enjoyed by fascism over the masses? Fascism is able to attract the masses because it demagogically appeals to their *most urgent needs and demands.* Fascism not only inflames prejudices that are deeply ingrained in the masses, but also plays on the better sentiments of the masses, on their sense of justice, and sometimes even on their revolutionary traditions. Why do the German fascists, those lackeys of the big bourgeoisie and mortal enemies of Socialism, represent themselves to the masses as "Socialists," and depict their accession to power as a "revolution"? Because they try to exploit the faith in revolution, the urge towards Socialism, which live in the hearts of the broad masses of the toilers of Germany.

Fascism acts in the interests of the extreme imperialists, but it presents itself to the masses in the guise of champion of an ill-treated nation, and appeals to outraged national sentiments, as German fascism did, for instance, when it won the support of the masses by the slogan "Against the Versailles Treaty!"

Fascism aims at the most unbridled exploitation of the masses, but it appeals to them with the most artful anti-capitalist demagogy, taking advantage of the profound hatred entertained by the toilers against the piratical bourgeoisie, the banks, trusts and the financial magnates, and advancing slogans which at the given moment are most alluring to the politically immature masses. In Germany: "The general welfare is higher than the welfare of the individual"; in Italy: "Our state is not a capitalist, but a corporate state"; in Japan: "For Japan, without exploitation"; in the United States: "Share the wealth," and so forth.

Fascism delivers up the people to be devoured by the most corrupt, most venal elements, but comes before the people with the demand for "an honest and incorruptible government." Speculating on the profound disillusionment of the masses in bourgeois-democratic government, fascism hypocritically denounces corruption (for instance, the Barmat and Sklarek affairs in Germany, the Stavisky affair in France, and numerous others).

It is in the interests of the most reactionary circles of the bourgeoisie that fascism intercepts the disappointed masses as they leave the old bourgeois parties. But it impresses these masses by the *severity of its attacks* on bourgeois governments and its irreconcilable attitude toward the old parties of the bourgeoisie.

Surpassing in its cynicism and hypocrisy all other varieties of bourgeois reaction, *fascism adapts* its demagogy to the national *peculiarities* of each country, and even to the peculiarities of the various social strata in one and the same country. And the petty-bourgeois masses, even a section of the workers, reduced to despair by want, unemployment and the insecurity of their existence, fall victim to the social and chauvinist demagogy of fascism.

Fascism comes to power as a *party of attack* on the revolutionary movement of the proletariat, on the masses of the people who are in a state of unrest; yet it stages its accession to power as a "revolutionary" movement against the bourgeoisie on behalf of "the whole nation" and for "the salvation" of the nation. (Let us recall Mussolini's "march" on Rome, Pilsudski's "march" on Warsaw, Hitler's National-Socialist "revolution" in Germany, and so forth.)

But whatever the masks which fascism adopts, whatever the

forms in which it presents itself, whatever the ways by which it comes to power:

Fascism is a most ferocious attack by capital on the toiling masses.

Fascism is unbridled chauvinism and annexationist war.

Fascism is rabid reaction and counter-revolution.

Fascism is the most vicious enemy of the working class and of all the toilers!

Georgi Dimitroff, "Report to the Seventh World Congress of the Communist International," *The United Front Against Fascism and War,* 1935, pp. 6-11.

C. Fascism – a Ferocious but Unstable Power

The fascist dictatorship of the bourgeoisie is a ferocious power but an unstable one.

What are the chief causes of the instability of the fascist dictatorship?

While fascism has undertaken to overcome the discord and antagonisms within the bourgeois camp, it is rendering these antagonisms even more acute. Fascism endeavors to establish its political monopoly by violently destroying other political parties. But the existence of the capitalist system, the existence of various classes and the accentuation of class contradictions inevitably tend to undermine and explode the political monopoly of fascism. This is not the case of a Soviet country, where the dictatorship of the proletariat is also realized by a party with a political monopoly, but where this political monopoly accords with the interests of millions of toilers and is increasingly being based on the construction of classless society. In a fascist country the party of the fascists cannot preserve its monopoly for long, because it cannot set itself the aim of abolishing classes and class contradictions. It puts an end to the legal existence of bourgeois parties. But a number of them continue to maintain an illegal existence, while the Communist Party, even in conditions of illegality, continues to make progress, becomes steeled and tempered and leads the struggle of the proletariat against the fascist dictatorship. Hence, under the blows of class contradictions, the political monopoly of fascism is bound to explode.

Another reason for the instability of the fascist dictatorship is that the contrast between the anti-capitalist demagogy of fascism and its policy of enriching the monopolist bourgeoisie in the most piratical fashion makes it easier to expose the class nature of fascism and tends to shake and narrow its mass basis.

Furthermore, the success of fascism arouses the profound hatred and indignation of the masses, helps to revolutionize them and provides a powerful stimulus for a united front of the proletariat against fascism.

By conducting a policy of economic nationalism (autarchy) and by seizing the greater portion of the national income for the purpose of preparing for war, fascism undermines the whole economic life of the country and accentuates the economic war between the capitalist states. It lends the conflicts that arise among the bourgeoisie the character of sharp and at times bloody collisions, which undermines the stability of the fascist state power in the eyes of the people. A government which murders its own followers, as was the case in Germany on June 30 of last year, a fascist government against which another section of the fascist bourgeoisie is conducting an armed fight (as exemplified by the National-Socialist *putsch* in Austria and the violent attacks of individual fascist groups on the fascist governments in Poland, Bulgaria, Finland and other countries) – a government of this character cannot for long maintain its authority in the eyes of the broad petty-bourgeois masses.

The working class must be able to take advantage of the antagonisms and conflicts within the bourgeois camp, but it must not cherish the illusion that fascism will exhaust itself of its own accord. Fascism will not collapse automatically. It is only the revolutionary activity of the working class which can help to take advantage of the conflicts which inevitably arise within the bourgeois camp in order to undermine the fascist dictatorship and to overthrow it.

By destroying the relics of bourgeois democracy, by elevating open violence to a system of government, fascism shakes democratic illusions and undermines the authority of the law in the eyes of the toiling masses. This is particularly the case in countries such as, for example, Austria and Spain, where the workers have taken up arms against fascism. In Austria, the heroic struggle of the Schutzbund and the Communists, in spite of their defeat, from the very outset shook the stability of the fascist dictatorship. In Spain, the bourgeoisie did not succeed in placing the fascist muzzle on the toilers. The armed straggles in Austria and Spain have resulted in ever wider masses of the working class coming to realize the necessity for a revolutionary class struggle.

Only such monstrous philistines, such lackeys of the bourgeoisie, as the superannuated theoretician of the Second International, Karl Kautsky, are capable of casting reproaches at the workers, to the effect that they should not have taken up arms in Austria and Spain. What would the working class movement in Austria and Spain look like to-day if the working class of these countries were guided by the treacherous counsels of the Kautskys? The working class would be experiencing profound demoralization in its ranks. Says Lenin:

> The school of civil war does not leave the people unaffected. It is a harsh school, and its complete curriculum *inevitably* includes the victories of the counter-revolution, the debaucheries of enraged reactionaries, savage punishments meted out by the old governments to the rebels, etc. But only downright pedants and mentally decrepit mummies can grieve over the fact that nations are entering this painful school; this school teaches the oppressed classes how to conduct civil war; it teaches how to bring about a victorious revolution; it concentrates in the masses of present-day slaves that hatred which is always harbored by the downtrodden, dull, ignorant slaves, and which leads those slaves who have become conscious of the shame of their slavery to the greatest historic exploits.[*]

The success of fascism in Germany has, as we know, been followed by a new wave of fascist onslaughts, which, in Austria, led to the provocation by Dollfuss, in Spain to the new onslaughts of the counter-revolutionaries on the revolutionary conquests of the masses, in Poland to the fascist reform of the constitution, while in France it spurred the armed detachments of the fascists to attempt a *coup d'état* in February 1934. But this victory, and the frenzy of the fascist dictatorship, called forth a counter-movement for a united proletarian front against fascism on an international scale. The burning of the Reichstag, which served as a signal for the general attack of fascism on the working class, the seizure and spoliation of the trade unions and the other working class organizations, the groans

---

[*] V. I. Lenin, "Inflammable Material in World Politics," *Selected Works,* Vol. IV, p. 298.

of the tortured anti-fascists rising from the vaults of the fascist barracks and concentration camps, are making clear to *the masses* the outcome of the reactionary, disruptive role played by the German Social-Democratic leaders, who rejected the proposal made by the Communists for a joint struggle against advancing fascism. The masses are becoming convinced of the necessity of amalgamating all the forces of the working class for the overthrow of fascism.

Hitler's victory also provided a decisive stimulus to the creation of a united front of the working class against fascism in France. Hitler's victory not only aroused in the workers the fear of the fate that befell the German workers, not only inflamed hatred for the executioners of their German class brothers, but also strengthened them in the determination that they would never, in any circumstances, allow the fate that befell the German working class to happen in their country.

The powerful urge towards the united front in all the capitalist countries shows that the lessons of defeat have not been in vain. The working class is beginning to act in a *new way.* The initiative shown by the Communist Party in the organization of the united front and the supreme self-sacrifice displayed by the Communists, by the revolutionary workers in the struggle against fascism, have resulted in an unprecedented increase in the prestige of the Communist International. At the same time, within the Second International, a profound crisis has been developing, which has manifested itself with particular clarity and has become particularly accentuated since the bankruptcy of German Social-Democracy.

The Social-Democratic workers are able to convince themselves ever more forcibly that fascist Germany, with all its horrors and barbarities, is in the final analysis *the result of the Social-Democratic policy of class collaboration with the bourgeoisie.* These masses are coming ever more clearly to realize that the path along which the German Social-Democratic leaders led the proletariat must not again be traversed. Never has there been such ideological dissension in the camp of the Second International as at the present time. A process of differentiation is taking place in all the Social-Democratic parties. Within their ranks *two principal* camps are forming: Side by side with the existing camp of reactionary elements, who are trying in every way to preserve the *bloc* between the Social-Democrats and the bourgeoisie, and who furiously reject a united front with the Communists, *there is beginning to form a camp of revolutionary elements who entertain doubts as to the correctness of the policy of class collaboration with the bourgeoisie, who are in favor of the creation of a united front with the Communists, and who are increasingly beginning to adopt the position of the revolutionary class struggle.*

Thus fascism, which appeared as the result of the decline of the capitalist system, in the long run acts as a factor of *its further disintegration.* Thus fascism, which has undertaken to bury Marxism, the revolutionary movement of the working class, is itself, as a result of the dialectics of life and the class struggle, leading to the further *development of those forces* which are bound to serve as fascism's grave-diggers, the gravediggers of capitalism.

Georgi Dimitroff, "Report to the Seventh World Congress of the Communist International," *The United, Front Against Fascism and War*, pp. 22-26.

D. Attitude of Communists Toward Bourgeois Democracy at the Present Stage

Lenski pointed out in his speech that "while mobilizing the masses to repel the onslaught of fascism against the rights of the toilers, the Polish Party at the same time had its misgivings about formulating positive democratic demands in order not to create democratic illusions among the masses." The Polish Party is, of course, not the only one in which such fear of formulating positive democratic demands exists in one way or another.

Where does that fear come from? It comes from an incorrect, non-dialectical conception of our attitude towards bourgeois democracy. We Communists are unswerving upholders of Soviet democracy, the great prototype of which is the proletarian dictatorship in the Soviet Union, where the introduction of equal suffrage, and of the direct and secret ballot is proclaimed by resolution of the Seventh Congress of Soviets at the same time that the last vestiges of bourgeois democracy are being wiped out in the capitalist countries. This Soviet democracy presupposes the victory of the proletarian revolution, the conversion of private property in the means of production into public property, the embarking of the overwhelming majority of the people on the road of Socialism. This democracy does not present a final form; it develops and will continue to develop in proportion as further progress is made in socialist construction, in the creation of classless society and in the overcoming of the survivals of capitalism in economic life and in the minds of the people.

But to-day the millions of toilers living under capitalism are faced with the necessity of taking a definite stand on *those forms* in which the *rule of the bourgeoisie* is clad in the various countries. We are not Anarchists and it is not at all a matter of indifference to us what kind of political regime exists in a given country: whether a bourgeois dictatorship in the form of bourgeois democracy, even with democratic rights and liberties greatly curtailed, or a bourgeois dictatorship in its open, fascist form. Being upholders of Soviet democracy, *we shall defend every inch of the democratic gains made by the working class in the course of years of stubborn struggle, and shall resolutely fight to extend these gains.*

How great were the sacrifices of the British working class before it secured the right to strike, a legal status for its trade unions, the right of assembly and freedom of the press, extension of the franchise, and other rights! How many tens of thousands of workers gave their lives in the revolutionary battles fought in France in the nineteenth century to obtain the elementary rights and the lawful opportunity of organizing their forces for the struggle against the exploiters! The proletariat of all countries has shed much of its blood to win bourgeois-democratic liberties, and will naturally fight with all its strength to retain them.

Our attitude toward bourgeois democracy is not the same under all conditions. For instance, at the time of the October Revolution, the Russian Bolsheviks engaged in a life-and-death struggle against all political parties which opposed the establishment of the proletarian dictatorship under the slogan of the defense of bourgeois democracy. The Bolsheviks fought these parties because the banner of bourgeois democracy had at that time become the standard around which all counter-revolutionary forces mobilized to challenge the victory of the proletariat. The situation is quite different in the capitalist countries at present. Now the fascist counter-revolution is attacking bourgeois democracy in an effort to establish a most barbaric regime of exploitation and suppression of the toiling masses. Now the toiling masses in a number of capitalist countries are faced with the necessity of making a *definite* choice, and of making it to-day, not between proletarian dictatorship and bourgeois democracy, but between bourgeois democracy and fascism.

Besides, we have now a situation which differs from that which existed, for example, in the epoch of capitalist stabilization. At that time the fascist danger was not as acute as it is to-day. At that time it was bourgeois dictatorship in the form of bourgeois democracy that the revolutionary workers were facing in a number of countries and it was against bourgeois democracy that they were concentrating their fire. In Germany, they fought against the Weimar Republic, not because it was a republic, but because it was a *bourgeois* republic, which was suppressing the revolutionary movement of the proletariat, especially in 1918-20 and in 1923.

But could the Communists maintain this stand also when the fascist movement began to raise its head, when, for instance, in 1932, the fascists in Germany were organizing and arming hundreds of thousands of storm troopers against the working class? Of course not. It was the mistake of the Communists in a number of countries, particularly in Germany, that they failed to take into account the changes which had taken place, but continued to repeat those slogans, maintain those tactical positions which had been correct a few years before, especially when the struggle for the proletarian dictatorship was an immediate issue, and when the entire German counter-revolution was rallying under the banner of the Weimar Republic, as it did in 1918-20.

And the circumstance that even to-day we must still call attention to that attitude in our ranks which fears to launch positive, democratic slogans indicates how little our comrades have mastered the Marxist-Leninist method of approaching such important problems of our tactics. Some say that the struggle for democratic rights may divert the workers from the struggle for the proletarian dictatorship. It may not be amiss to recall what Lenin said on this question:

> ...It would be a fundamental mistake to suppose that the struggle for democracy can divert the proletariat from the Socialist revolution, or obscure, or overshadow it, etc. On the contrary, just as Socialism cannot be victorious unless it introduces complete democracy, so the proletariat will be unable to prepare for victory over the bourgeoisie unless it wages a many-sided, consistent and revolutionary struggle for democracy.*

---

* V. I. Lenin, "The Socialist Revolution and the Right of Nations to Self-Determination," *Selected Works,* Vol. V, p. 268.

These words should be firmly fixed in the memories of all our comrades, bearing in mind that the great revolutions in history have grown out of small movements for the defense of the elementary rights of the working class. But in order to be able to link up the struggle for democratic rights with the struggle of the working class for Socialism, it is necessary first and foremost to discard any cut-and-dried approach to the question of defense of bourgeois democracy.

Georgi Dimitroff, "Report to the Seventh World Congress of the Communist International," *The United Front Against Fascism and War,* pp. 106-110.

II. THE DICTATORSHIP OF THE PROLETARIAT
AND ITS THREE MAIN ASPECTS

1. Historical Necessity of the Dictatorship of the Proletariat

...Between capitalist and communist society lies a
period of revolutionary transformation from one to the
other. There corresponds also to this a political transition
period during which the state can be nothing else than the
revolutionary dictatorship of the proletariat.[*]

A. Stalin on the Marxist-Leninist Teaching of the Dictatorship of the
Proletariat as a Weapon of the Proletarian Revolution

...The question of the proletarian dictatorship is above all a
question of the basic content of the proletarian revolution. The proletarian revolution, its movement, its sweep and its achievements,
acquire flesh and blood only through the dictatorship of the proletariat. The dictatorship of the proletariat is the weapon of the proletarian revolution, its organ, its most important stronghold which is
called into being, first, to crush the resistance of the overthrown
exploiters and to consolidate its achievements; secondly, to lead the
proletarian revolution to its completion, to lead the revolution on-
ward to the complete victory of socialism. Victory over the bourgeoisie and the overthrow of its power may be gained by revolution
even without the dictatorship of the proletariat. But the revolution
will not be in a position to crush the resistance of the bourgeoisie,
maintain its victory and move on to the decisive victory for socialism, unless at a certain stage of its development it creates a special
organ in the form of the dictatorship of the proletariat as its principal bulwark.

"The question of power is the fundamental question of the revolution." (Lenin.) Does this mean that the only thing required is to
assume power, to seize it? No, it does not. The seizure of power is
only the beginning. For a number of reasons, the bourgeoisie overthrown in one country for a considerable time remains stronger than
the proletariat which has overthrown it. Therefore, the important
thing is to retain power, to consolidate it and make it invincible.
What is required to attain this end? At least three main tasks con-

---

[*] Karl Marx, *Critique of the Gotha Programme,* London and New
York, 1933, pp. 44-45.

36

fronting the dictatorship of the proletariat "on the morrow" of victory must be fulfilled. They are:

a. to break the resistance of the landlords and capitalists overthrown and expropriated by the revolution, and to liquidate every attempt they make to restore the power of capital;

b. to organize construction in such a way as will rally all toilers around the proletariat and to carry on this work in such a way as will prepare for the liquidation, the extinction of classes;

c. to arm the revolution and to organize the army of the revolution for the struggle against the external enemy and for the struggle against imperialism.

The dictatorship of the proletariat is necessary in order to carry out and fulfill these tasks.

> The transition from capitalism to communism (Lenin says), represents an entire historical epoch. Until this epoch has terminated, the exploiters will inevitably cherish the hope of restoration, and this *hope* will be converted into *attempts* at restoration. And after their first serious defeat, the overthrown exploiters – who had not expected their overthrow, who never believed it possible, who would not permit the thought of it – will throw themselves with tenfold energy, with furious passion and hatred grown a hundredfold into the battle for the recovery of their lost "paradise" on behalf of their families who had been leading such a sweet and easy life and whom now the "common herd" is condemning to ruin and destitution (or to "common" work).... In the wake of the capitalist exploiters will be found the broad masses of the petty bourgeoisie, to whose vacillation and hesitation the historical experience of every country for decades bears witness; one day they march behind the proletariat, the next day they will take fright at the difficulties of the revolution, become panic-stricken at the first defeat or semi-defeat of the workers; they become irritable, they run about, snivel and rush from one camp to the other. (*The Proletarian Revolution and Renegade Kautsky,* chap. III.)

Now the bourgeoisie has reasons for making attempts at restoration, because for a long time after its overthrow it remains stronger than the proletariat which has overthrown it.

If the exploiters (Lenin says), are vanquished in only a single country, which, of course, is the typical case since a simultaneous revolution in a number of countries is a rare exception, they *still remain stronger* than the exploited. (*Ibid.*)

Wherein lies the strength of the overthrown bourgeoisie? First:

In the strength of international capital, in the strength and durability of the international connections of the bourgeoisie. (*"Left-Wing" Communism: An Infantile Disorder.*)

Secondly:

In the fact that "for a long time after the revolution, the exploiters will inevitably retain a number of enormous and real advantages: they will have money left (it is impossible to abolish money all at once), some movable property, often of considerable value; there remain their connections, their organizing and administrative ability and the knowledge of all the secrets of administration (of usages, of procedure, of ways and means, of possibilities); there remain their superior education, their kinship to the highest ranks of the technical personnel (who live and think like the bourgeoisie); there remains their immeasurable superiority in the art of war (this is very important), etc., etc." (*The Proletarian Revolution and Renegade Kautsky,* chap. III.)

Thirdly:

In the force of habit, in the strength of *small-scale production.* For unfortunately, very, very much of small-scale production still remains in the world, and small-scale production *gives birth* to capitalism and the bourgeoisie continuously, daily, hourly, spontaneously, and on a mass scale.... (*"Left-Wing" Communism: An Infantile Disorder.*)

Fourthly:

The abolition of classes not only means driving out the landlords and capitalists – that we accomplished with comparative ease – it means also *getting rid of the small commodity producers,* and they *cannot be driven out* or crushed; we must live in harmony with them; they can (and must) be remolded and reeducated, but this can be done only by very prolonged, slow, cautious organizational work. (*Ibid.*)

That is why Lenin declares:

The dictatorship of the proletariat is the fiercest, most acute and most merciless war of the new class against the *more powerful enemy,* against the bourgeoisie, whose resistance is increased *tenfold* by its overthrow, [that] the dictatorship of the proletariat is a persistent struggle – sanguinary and bloodless, violent and peaceful, military and economic, educational and administrative, against the forces and traditions of the old society. (*Ibid.*)

It need hardly be emphasized that there is not the slightest possibility of accomplishing these tasks in a short period of time, within a few years. We must, therefore, regard the dictatorship of the proletariat, the transition from capitalism to communism, not as a fleeting period replete with "super-revolutionary" deeds and decrees, but as an entire historical epoch full of civil wars and external conflicts, of persistent organizational work and economic construction, of attacks and retreats, of victories and defeats. This historical epoch is necessary not only in order to create the economic and cultural prerequisites for the complete victory of socialism, but also in order to enable the proletariat, first, to educate itself and become steeled into a force capable of governing the country; secondly, to re-educate and remold the petty-bourgeois strata along such lines as will assure the organization of socialist production.

Marx said to the workers:

You will have to go through fifteen, twenty, fifty years of civil wars and conflicts of peoples, not only to change the conditions, but in order to change yourselves and to make yourselves capable of wielding political power.

Developing Marx's thought still further, Lenin goes on to say:

"Under the dictatorship of the proletariat we will have to reeducate millions of peasants and petty proprietors, hundreds of thousands of employees, officials and bourgeois intellectuals; to subordinate all these to the proletarian state and to proletarian leadership; to overcome their bourgeois habits and traditions"... just as much as it will be necessary... "to reeducate in a protracted struggle, on the basis of the dictatorship of the proletariat, the proletarians themselves, who do not abandon their petty-bourgeois prejudices at one stroke, by a miracle, at the behest of the Virgin Mary, at the behest of a slogan, resolution or decree, but only in the course of a long and difficult mass struggle against mass petty-bourgeois influences." (*Ibid.*)

Joseph Stalin, *Leninism,* Vol. I, pp. 41-44.

B. Marx and Lenin on the Dictatorship of the Proletariat as an Historically Necessary Transition Stage from Capitalism to Communism

In a feuilleton published in your issue of June 22, of the current year, you reproached me for defending the rule and the *dictatorship of the working class,* while in contrast to myself, you advocated the *abolition of all* class *distinctions.* I do not understand this emendation.

You know well that in the *Manifesto of the Communist Party* (published before the February Revolution of 1848) on page 16 it is said: "If the proletariat, during its contest with the bourgeoisie is compelled, by the force of circumstances, to organize itself as a class; if, by means of a revolution, it makes itself the ruling class, and, as such sweeps away by force the old conditions of production, then it will, along with these conditions, have swept away the conditions for the existence of class antagonism and of classes generally, and will thereby have abolished its own supremacy as a class."

You know that before February 1848, in the *Poverty of Philosophy,* I defended this very point of view against Proudhon.

Finally, in the same article which you criticize (third issue of the *Neue Rheinische Zeitung,* page 32) it is said: "This Socialism (*i.e.,* Communism) means the proclamation of the permanent revolution, the class dictatorship of the proletariat as the necessary transition stage to the abolition of all class distinctions, the abolition of all production relations on which these distinctions rest, the abolition of all social relations which correspond to these production relations, to a revolution in all ideas which spring from these social relations."

Karl Marx and Frederick Engels, *Works,* Russian edition, Preface to Vol. VIII, Karl Marx's "Letter to the Editor of the *Neue Deutsche Zeitung,*" June 1850.

In 1907, Mehring, in the magazine *Die Neue Zeit* (Vol. XXV, 2, p. 164) published extracts from a letter from Marx to Weydemeyer dated March 5, 1852. This letter among other things, contains the following remarkable observation:

> And now as to myself, no credit is due to me for discovering the existence of classes in modern society nor yet the struggle between them. Long before me, bourgeois historians had described the historical development of this class struggle, and bourgeois economists, the economic anatomy of the classes. What I did that was new was to prove: (1) that the *existence of classes* is only bound up with *particular historical phases in the development of production* (*historische Entwicklungsphasen der Produktion*); (2) that the class struggle necessarily leads to the *dictatorship of the proletariat;* (3) that this dictatorship itself only constitutes the transition to the *abolition of all classes and to a classless society.*[*]

In these words Marx succeeded in expressing with striking clarity, first, the chief and radical differences between his doctrine and those of the most advanced and most profound thinkers of the bourgeoisie; and second, the essence of his doctrine of the state.

It is often said and written that the core of Marx's theory is the class struggle; but it is not true. And from this error, very often springs the opportunist distortion of Marxism, its falsification to make it acceptable to the bourgeoisie. The theory of the class struggle *was* not created by Marx, but by the bourgeoisie *before* Marx, and generally speaking, it is *acceptable* to the bourgeoisie. Those who recognize *only* the class struggle are not yet Marxists; those may be found to have gone no further than the boundaries of bourgeois reasoning and bourgeois politics. To limit Marxism to the theory of the class struggle means curtailing Marxism – distorting it, reducing it to something which is acceptable to the bourgeoisie. A Marxist is one who *extends* the acceptance of the class struggle to

---

[*] Karl Marx and Frederick Engels, *Correspondence,* London and New York, 1984, p. 57. – *Ed.*

the acceptance of the *dictatorship of the proletariat*. This is where the profound difference lies, between a Marxist and an ordinary petty (and even big) bourgeois. This is the touchstone on which the *real* understanding and acceptance of Marxism should be tested. And it is not surprising that, when the history of Europe brought the working class face to face with this question in a *practical* way, not only all the opportunists and reformists, but all the Kautskyists (those who vacillate between reformism and Marxism) proved to be miserable philistines and petty-bourgeois democrats, who repudiated the dictatorship of the proletariat. Kautsky's pamphlet, *The Dictatorship of the Proletariat,* published in August 1918, *i.e.,* long after the first edition of the present pamphlet, is an example of the petty-bourgeois distortion of Marxism and base renunciation of it *in practice,* while hypocritically recognizing it in words. (See my pamphlet, *The Proletarian Revolution and Renegade Kautsky.*)

Present-day opportunism in the person of its principal representative, the ex-Marxist, K. Kautsky, fits in completely with Marx's characterization of the bourgeois position as quoted above, for this opportunism limits the field of recognition of the class struggle to the realm of bourgeois relationships. (Within this realm, within its framework, not a single educated liberal will refuse to recognize the class struggle "in principle!") Opportunism *does not carry* the recognition of class struggle to its main point, to the period of *transition* from capitalism to communism, to the period of the overthrow and complete abolition of the bourgeoisie. In reality, this period inevitably becomes a period of unusually violent class struggles in their sharpest possible form and, therefore, during this period the state must inevitably be a state that is democratic *in a new way* (for the proletariat and the propertyless in general) and dictatorial *in a new way* (against the bourgeoisie).

To proceed. The essence of Marx's doctrine of the state is assimilated only by those who understand that the dictatorship of a *single* class is necessary not only for class society in general, not only for the *proletariat* which has overthrown the bourgeoisie, but for the entire *historical period* between capitalism and "classless society," Communism. The forms of the bourgeois state are extremely varied, but in essence they are all the same: in one way or another, in the last analysis, all these states are inevitably the *dictatorship of the bourgeoisie.* The transition from capitalism to communism will certainly create a great variety and abundance of political forms, but in essence there will inevitably be only one: *the dictatorship of the proletariat.*

V. I. Lenin, *The State and Revolution*, pp. 29-31.

2. Three Main Aspects of the Dictatorship of the Proletariat

A. Stalin on the Main Tasks of the Proletarian Revolution and the Three Aspects of the Dictatorship of the Proletariat

What are the characteristic features that distinguish the proletarian revolution from the bourgeois revolution?

The differences between the two may be reduced to five basic points.

1. The bourgeois revolution usually begins when more or less finished forms of the capitalist order already exist, forms which have grown and ripened within the womb of feudal society prior to the open revolution; whereas the proletarian revolution begins at a time when finished forms of the socialist order are either absent, or almost completely absent.

2. The fundamental task of the bourgeois revolution reduces itself to seizing power and operating that power in conformity with the already existing bourgeois economy; whereas the main task of the proletarian revolution reduces itself to building up the new socialist economy after having seized power.

3. The bourgeois revolution is usually completed with the seizure of power; whereas for the proletarian revolution the seizure of power is only its *beginning,* while power is used as a lever for the transformation of the old economy and for the organization of the new one.

4. The bourgeois revolution limits itself to substituting one group of exploiters by another in the seat of power, and therefore has no need to destroy the old state machine; whereas the proletarian revolution removes all groups of exploiters from power, and places in power the leader of all the toilers and exploited, the class of proletarians, and therefore it cannot avoid destroying the old state machine and replacing it by a new one.

The bourgeois revolution cannot for any length of time rally the millions of the toiling and exploited masses around the bourgeoisie, for the very reason that they are toilers and exploited; whereas the proletarian revolution can and must link them up precisely as toilers and exploited in a durable alliance with the proletariat, if it wishes to carry out its fundamental task of consolidating the power of the proletariat and building the new socialist economy.

Here are some of Lenin's fundamental postulates on the subject:

> One of the basic differences between the bourgeois revolution and the socialist revolution (says Lenin) is that, in the case of the bourgeois revolution, which grows out of feudalism, the new economic organizations are gradually created within the womb of the old order, and by degrees modify all the aspects of feudal society. The bourgeois revolution had but one task to perform: to sweep away, to fling aside, to destroy all the fetters of the previous society. Fulfilling this task, every bourgeois revolution fulfills all that is demanded of it: it stimulates the growth of capitalism. But the socialist revolution is in an altogether different position. The more backward the country in which, thanks to the zigzag course of history, the socialist revolution has to be begun, the more difficult for it is the transition from the old capitalist relations to socialist relations. Here, to the tasks of destruction there are added new organizational tasks of unheard-of difficulty.... (*Collected Works,* Russian edition, Vol. XXII, p. 315.)

> If the creative force of the masses, in the Russian revolution (continues Lenin), which went through the great experience of the year 1905, had not created soviets already in February 1917, then these soviets could not under any circumstances have seized power in October, for success depended upon the existence of finished organizational forms of a movement that embraced millions of people. The soviets were such a finished organizational form, and that is why the striking successes and triumphal procession that we experienced awaited us in the political field, for the new political form was ready at hand, and all we had to do was by a few decrees to transform the Soviet power from the embryonic condition in which it existed during the first months of the revolution, into a form legally recognized and confirmed in the Russian state – the Russian Soviet republic. (*Ibid.*)

> There still remained (says Lenin) two tasks of enormous difficulty, the solution of which could, under no circumstances, be the same triumphal procession that our rev-

olution was.... (*Ibid.*)

First, there was the task of internal organization which faces every socialist revolution. The difference between the socialist revolution and the bourgeois revolution is precisely that, in the latter case, finished forms of capitalist relationships already exist, whereas the Soviet power, the proletarian power, does not get these relationships, if we leave out of account the most developed forms of capitalism which, as a matter of fact, embraced only a few peaks of industry and affected agriculture only to a very slight extent. The organization of accounting, the control over large-scale enterprises, the transformation of the whole state economic mechanism into a single great machine, into an economic organism which shall work in such a way that hundreds of millions of people shall be directed by a single plan, such is the tremendous organizational task which lay on our shoulders. Under the existing conditions of labor it under no circumstances allowed solution in the "hurrah" fashion in which we were able to solve the problems of the civil war.... (*Ibid.*, p. 316.)

The second enormous difficulty was... the international question. If we were able to cope so easily with Kerensky's bands, if we so easily established our power, if the decree on the socialization of the land, and on workers' control, was secured without the slightest difficulty – if we obtained all this so easily it was only because for a brief space of time a fortunate combination of circumstances protected us from international imperialism. International imperialism, with all the might of its capital and its highly organized military technique, which represents a real force, a real fortress of international capital, could under no circumstances, under no possible conditions, live side by side with the Soviet republic, both because of its objective situation and because of the economic interests of the capitalist class which was incorporated in it, could not do this because of commercial ties and of international financial relationships. A conflict is inevitable. This is the greatest difficulty of the Russian revolution, its greatest historical problem: the necessity to solve international problems, the necessity to call forth the world revolution. (*Ibid.*, p. 317.)

Such is the inner character and the basic idea of the proletarian revolution.

Can such a radical transformation of the old bourgeois system of society be achieved without a violent revolution, without the dictatorship of the proletariat?

Obviously not. To think that such a revolution can be carried out peacefully within the framework of bourgeois democracy, which is adapted to the domination of the bourgeoisie, means one of two things. It means either madness, and the loss of normal human understanding, or else an open and gross repudiation of the proletarian revolution....

...Now, if it be admitted that the dictatorship of the proletariat is the basic content of the proletarian revolution, what then are the fundamental characteristics of the dictatorship of the proletariat?

Here is the most general definition of the dictatorship of the proletariat, given by Lenin:

> The dictatorship of the proletariat is not the end of the class struggle but its continuation in new forms. The dictatorship of the proletariat is the class struggle of the proletariat, which has achieved victory and has seized political power, against the bourgeoisie who have been defeated but not annihilated, who have not disappeared, who have not ceased their resistance, who have increased their resistance. (*Collected Works,* Russian edition, Vol. XXIV, p. 311.)

Replying to those who confuse the dictatorship of the proletariat with "popular," "elected" and "non-class" government, Lenin states:

> The class that has seized political power has done so, conscious of the fact that it has seized power alone. This is implicit in the concept of the dictatorship of the proletariat. This concept has meaning only when one class knows that it alone takes political power into its own hands, and does not deceive either itself or others by talk about popular, elected government, sanctified by the whole people. (*Collected Works,* Russian edition, Vol. XXVI, p. 286.)

This does not mean, however, that the rule of this one class, the class of the proletarians, which does not and cannot share this rule with any other class, does not need an alliance with the toiling and exploited masses of other classes for the attainment of its objectives. On the contrary. This rule, the rule of a single class, can be firmly established and exercised to the full only by means of a special form of alliance between the class of proletarians and the toiling masses of the petty-bourgeois classes, especially the toiling masses of the peasantry.

What is this special form of alliance? What does it consist of? Does not this alliance with the toiling masses of other, non-proletarian classes generally contradict the idea of the dictatorship of one class?

This special form of alliance lies in that the leading force of this alliance is the proletariat, that the leader in the state, the leader within the system of the dictatorship of the proletariat is *a single* party, the party of the proletariat, the party of the Communists, which *does not and cannot share* that leadership with other parties.

As you see, the contradiction is only an apparent, a seeming one.

> The dictatorship of the proletariat (Lenin says) is a *special form of class alliance* (My italics. – *J. S.*) between the proletariat, the vanguard of the toilers, and the numerous non-proletarian strata of toilers (the petty bourgeoisie, the small masters, the peasantry, the intelligentsia, etc.), or the majority of these; it is an alliance against capital, an alliance aiming at the complete overthrow of capital, at the complete suppression of the resistance of the bourgeoisie and of any attempt on their part at restoration, an alliance aiming at the final establishment and consolidation of socialism. It is a special type of alliance, which is being built up under special circumstances, namely, in the circumstances of furious civil war; it is an alliance between the firm supporters of socialism and its wavering allies and sometimes neutrals (when the agreement to fight becomes an agreement to maintain neutrality). It is an alliance between classes which differ economically, politically, socially and ideologically. (*Collected Works*, Russian edition, Vol. XXIV, p. 311.)

In one of his instructional reports, Comrade Kamenev, disputing such a conception of the dictatorship of the proletariat, states:

> The dictatorship *is not* an alliance between one class

and another. (*Pravda,* January 14, 1925.)

I believe that Comrade Kamenev had in view, above all, a passage in my pamphlet *The October Revolution and the Tactics of the Russian Communists,* where it is stated:

> The dictatorship of the proletariat is not simply the governing upper stratum "cleverly" "selected" by the careful hand of an "experienced strategist," and "sensibly" relying on the support of one section or another of the population. The dictatorship of the proletariat is a class alliance between the proletariat and the toiling masses of the peasantry, for the purpose of overthrowing capital, for bringing about the final victory of socialism, an alliance based on the condition that its leading force is the proletariat.

I completely endorse this formulation of the dictatorship of the proletariat, for I think that it wholly and fully corresponds to Lenin's formulation, just quoted.

I maintain that Comrade Kamenev's declaration that "the dictatorship *is not* an alliance between one class and another," in the categorical form in which it is made, has nothing in common with the Leninist theory of the dictatorship of the proletariat.

I maintain that only those who have never understood the meaning of the idea of the bond,[*] the idea of the alliance between the workers and the peasants, the idea of the *hegemony* of the proletariat within this alliance, can speak in such a fashion.

Such statements can only be made by those who have failed to grasp Lenin's thesis that:

> *Nothing but an agreement with the peasants* (My italics. – *J. S.*) can save the socialist revolution in Russia until the revolution has taken place in other countries. (*Collected Works,* Russian edition, Vol. XXVI, p. 238.)

Such statements can only be made by those who have failed to grasp Lenin's proposition that:

> *The supreme principle of the dictatorship* (My italics. – *J. S.*) is the preservation of the alliance between the proletariat and the peasantry, in order that the proletariat may re-

---

[*] The word used in Russian is *smychka. – Ed.*

tain the leading role and state power. (*Ibid.,* p. 460.)

Pointing to one of the most important aims of the dictatorship, namely, the suppression of the exploiters, Lenin states:

> The scientific concept, dictatorship, means nothing more nor less than power that directly rests on violence, that is not limited by any laws or restricted by any absolute rules.... Dictatorship means – note this once and for all, Messrs. Cadets[*] – unlimited power, resting on violence and not on law. During civil war, victorious power can only be dictatorship. (*Collected Works,* Russian edition, Vol. XXV, pp. 436 and 444.)

But, of course, the dictatorship of the proletariat does not merely mean violence, although there is no dictatorship without violence.

> Dictatorship (says Lenin) does not mean violence alone, although it is impossible without violence. It likewise signifies a higher organization of labor than that which previously existed. (*Collected Works*, Russian edition, Vol. XXIV, p. 305.)

> The dictatorship of the proletariat is not merely the use of violence against the exploiters, and is not even mainly the use of violence. The economic basis of this revolutionary violence, the guarantee of its vitality and success, is that the proletariat represents and introduces a higher type of social organization of labor compared with capitalism. That is the essential point. This is the source of the strength of Communism and the guarantee of its inevitable complete victory. (*Ibid.,* p. 335.)

> Its quintessence (*i.e.,* of the dictatorship – *J. S.*) lies in the organization and discipline of the advanced detachment of the toilers, of its vanguard, its sole leader, the proletariat. Its aim is to establish socialism, to put an end to the division of society into classes, to make all members of society toilers, to remove the soil for the exploitation of man by man. This aim cannot be achieved at one stroke. It demands quite a protracted period of transition from capitalism to socialism, because the reorganization of production is a dif-

---

[*] The Constitutional Democrats – *Ed.*

ficult matter, because time is needed for radical changes in all spheres of life, and because the enormous force of habit of petty-bourgeois and bourgeois management can be overcome only by a long stubborn struggle. That was why Marx spoke of the dictatorship of the proletariat as of a whole period, a period of transition from capitalism to socialism. (*Ibid.,* p. 314.)

Such are the characteristic features of the dictatorship of the proletariat.

Hence there are three fundamental aspects of the dictatorship of the proletariat.

1. The utilization of the power of the proletariat for the suppression of the exploiters, for the defense of the country, for the consolidation of the ties with the proletarians of other lands, and for the development and the victory of the revolution in all countries.

2. The utilization of the power of the proletariat in order to detach the toiling and exploited masses once and for all from the bourgeoisie, to consolidate the alliance of the proletariat with these masses, to enlist these masses for the work of socialist construction, and to insure the state leadership of these masses by the proletariat.

3. The utilization of the power of the proletariat for the organization of socialism, for the abolition of classes, and for the transition to a society without classes, to a society without a state.

The dictatorship of the proletariat is a combination of all three aspects. None of these three aspects can be advanced as the *sole* characteristic feature of the dictatorship of the proletariat. On the other hand, it is sufficient for but one of these three characteristic features to be lacking, for the dictatorship of the proletariat to cease being a dictatorship in a capitalist encirclement. Therefore not one of these three features can be omitted without running the risk of distorting the concept of the dictatorship of the proletariat. Only all these three features taken together give us a complete and fully rounded concept of the dictatorship of the proletariat.

The dictatorship of the proletariat has its periods, its special forms, its diversified methods of work. During the period of civil war, the coercive aspect of the dictatorship is especially conspicuous. But it by no means follows from this that no constructive work is carried on during the period of civil war. The civil war itself cannot be waged without constructive work. On the other hand, during the period of socialist construction, the peaceful, organizational and cultural work of the dictatorship, revolutionary law, etc., are especially conspicuous. But here, again, it by no means follows that during the period of construction, the coercive side of the dictatorship has fallen away, or could do so. The organs of suppression, the army and other organizations are as necessary now in the period of construction as they were during the civil war period. Without these institutions, constructive work by the dictatorship with any degree of security would be impossible. It should not be forgotten that for the time being the revolution has been victorious in only one country. It should not be forgotten that as long as we live in a capitalist encirclement, so long will the danger of intervention, with all the resultant consequences, continue.

Joseph Stalin, *Leninism,* Vol. I, pp. 266-69; 270-74.

...The dictatorship of the proletariat is not only *violence.* It is also the leadership of the toiling masses of the non-proletarian classes, it is also the *building up* of socialist economy, which is of a higher type than capitalist economy, and has a greater productivity of labor than capitalist economy. The dictatorship of the proletariat is: 1: *In regard to the capitalists and landowners,* the exercise of violence, unrestricted by law; 2: *in regard to the peasantry,* the leadership of the proletariat; 3: *in regard to society as a whole,* the building of socialism.

Not one of these aspects can be left out without distorting the concept of the dictatorship of the proletariat. Only these three aspects taken together give a complete and finished concept of the dictatorship of the proletariat.

Ibid., p. 220.

B. The Dictatorship of the Proletariat Is Not the End but the Continuation of the Proletarian Class Struggle in New Forms

1. The main source from which springs the "socialists'" lack of understanding of the proletarian dictatorship is their failure to follow up the idea of the class struggle to the end....

The dictatorship of the proletariat is the *continuation* of the proletarian class struggle in *new* forms. This is the crux of the matter and this they fail to understand.

The proletariat as a *particular* class *continues* to carry on its class struggle alone.

2. The state is merely = the *instrument* of the proletariat in its class struggle. A particular *club* and nothing more.

The old prejudices concerning the state (*cf. State and Revolution*). The new forms of the state constitute the theme of Part C. This is only an *approach* to it.

3. Under the dictatorship of the proletariat the forms of the proletarian class struggle cannot be the old ones. *Five* new main tasks and corresponding new forms:

4. (1) *The suppression of the resistance of the exploiters.* This as the task (and content) of the epoch, is altogether lost sight of by the opportunists and the "socialists."

The resistance of the exploiters begins *before* and *grows more acute* after their overthrow, from two sides. A fight to *a finish* or "talky-talky" like the petty bourgeoisie and the "socialists".

Hence –

($\alpha\alpha$) The particular (extreme) severity of the class struggle.

($\beta\beta$) The new forms of resistance which correspond to capitalism and its higher stage (conspiracies ÷ sabotage ÷ influence exercised upon the petty bourgeoisie, etc.).

And in particular –

5. (2) ($\gamma\gamma$) *Civil war.* Revolution in general and civil war (1649, 1793), compare *Karl Kautsky, 1902, in Social Revolution.*

Civil war in the period of the international ties of capitalism.

Civil war and the "abolition" of the party (Karl Kautsky). Terror and civil war.

Converting imperialist war into civil war. (The ignorance and low cowardice of the "socialists.")

Compare Marx 1870: to teach the proletariat to wield arms. *The period* of 1871-1914 and *the period* of civil wars.

α) Russia, Hungary, Finland, Germany.

β) Switzerland and America.

γ) The inevitability of combining civil war with revolutionary wars (compare the program of the Russian Communist Party).

"The ruling class." Domination excludes "freedom and equality."

6. (3) *"Neutralizing" the petty bourgeoisie, particularly the peasantry.*

The *Communist Manifesto* (reactionary and revolutionary "in proportion as").

Karl Kautsky in his *Agrarian Question.* Neutralization, under the pretext of improving upon it, this idea has been debased.

"Neutralization" in practice, holding down by violence (Engels 1895).

Example:

Persuasion, etc., etc.

Enlisting + holding down, "in proportion as."

"To lead," "to guide," "to inspire and lead," the class meaning of conceptions.

Peasant and worker.

The peasant as a toiler and the peasant as an exploiter (a profiteer, a proprietor).

"In proportion as." Waverings during the struggle. The *experience* of the struggle.

"One reactionary mass": Engels 1875, attitude towards the *Commune.*

7. (4) *"Utilizing" the bourgeoisie.*

"The experts." Not only suppression of resistance, not only "neutralization," but also giving employment, pressing into the service of the proletariat.

Compare the program of the Russian

Communist Party – "military experts."

8. (5) *Training in a new discipline.*

(α) The dictatorship of the proletariat and trade unions.

(β) "The Communist Subbotniks."

(γ) The purging of the Party and its role.

(δ) Premiums and piece work.

V. I. Lenin, *Collected Works,* Russian edition, Volume XXV, pp. 5-7. (Fragment of a manuscript, one of five, representing rough drafts of a pamphlet conceived by Lenin in 1919, which, however, was never written.)

C. Lenin's Evaluation of the Dictatorship of the Proletariat as the Suppression of the Resistance of the Bourgeoisie, as the Leader of the Petty Bourgeois Toiling Masses as well as the Instrument for the Building Up of Socialism

The dictatorship of the proletariat is not the end of the class struggle but its continuation in new forms. The dictatorship of the proletariat is the class struggle of the victorious proletariat that has taken the political power into its own hands against the bourgeoisie which, though defeated, is not yet destroyed, has not yet disappeared, has not stopped its resistance, but even increased it. The dictatorship of the proletariat is a special form of the class alliance between the proletariat, the vanguard of the toilers, and the numerous non-proletarian strata of the toilers (petty bourgeoisie, petty proprietors, the peasantry, the intellectuals, etc.) or their majority; an alliance against capital, an alliance for the complete overthrow of capital, complete suppression of the resistance of the bourgeoisie and their attempts at restoration; an alliance for the purpose of fully establishing and consolidating socialism. It is a particular kind of alliance, formed in a particular situation, namely, in a situation of fierce civil war; it is an alliance of the staunch adherents of Socialism with its wavering allies, sometimes with "neutrals" (when, from a militant agreement the alliance is converted into a neutrality agreement); an alliance between classes which are economically, politically, socially and morally unequal. It is only the rotten heroes of the rotten "Bern" or yellow International, men like Kautsky, Martov and Co. who instead of studying the concrete forms, conditions and tasks of this alliance, confine themselves to general

54

phrases about "freedom," "equality" and "unity of labor democracy," *i.e.,* scraps from the ideological armory of the period of commodity economy. (Lenin, *Collected Works,* Russian edition, Vol. XXIV, p. 311.)

However, it is not mere force and not chiefly force that is the essence of the proletarian dictatorship. Its main essence is the organization and discipline of the advanced detachment of the toilers, its vanguard, its sole leader, the proletariat. The object of the proletarian dictatorship is to create socialism, to abolish the division of society in classes, to turn all the members of society into toilers, to eliminate all possibilities for the exploitation of man by man. This object cannot be accomplished all at once, it requires a pretty long period of transition from capitalism to socialism, because reorganization of production is difficult, because radical changes in all spheres of life require time, and because the great force of habit to conduct affairs in a petty bourgeois and bourgeois manner may be overcome only by prolonged and obstinate struggle. That is why Marx speaks of a whole period of the dictatorship of the proletariat as the period of transition from capitalism to socialism.

Throughout this transition period resistance will be offered to the revolution by the capitalists and their numerous followers from among the bourgeois intellectuals whose resistance is premeditative as well as by the great mass of toilers, including peasants, who are too much overwhelmed by petty bourgeois habits and traditions and whose resistance is often unintentional. Among these sections waverings are inevitable. The peasant as a toiler strives for socialism, preferring the dictatorship of the workers to the dictatorship of the bourgeoisie. The peasant as the seller of corn hankers after the bourgeoisie, after free trade, *i.e.,* he harks back to old "habitual," "primordial" capitalism.

The dictatorship of the proletariat, the rule of one class, the force of its organization and discipline, its centralized power based on all the acquisitions of culture, science and capitalist technique, its proletarian kinship to the psychology of every toiler, its authority in the eyes of the isolated toiler in the village or in petty industry who is not so developed and not so firm in politics, that is what is needed in order that the proletariat *may* lead the peasantry and the petty bourgeois strata in general. Here phrases about "democracy" in general, "unity" or "unity of labor democracy," "equality" of all "the men of toil" and so on and so forth – phrases which the social-chauvinists and the Kautskyists who have grown philistine are so fond of – won't help. Phrase-mongering only throws dust in the eyes, beclouds the consciousness and perpetuates the old stupidity, conservatism and routine of capitalism, parliamentarism and bourgeois democracy.

The abolition of classes is a matter of long, difficult, stubborn *class struggle* which, after the overthrow of the power of capital, *after* the destruction of the bourgeois state, *after* the establishment of the dictatorship of the proletariat, does *not disappear* (as the vulgar people of the old socialism and of the old Social-Democracy imagine), but only changes its forms and in many respects grows fiercer still.

The proletariat must maintain its power, strengthen its organizing influence, "neutralize" those sections which are afraid of parting company with the bourgeoisie and too hesitatingly follow the proletariat, by waging the class struggle against the resistance of the bourgeoisie, against conservatism, routine, indecision, and the waverings of the petty bourgeoisie; it must consolidate the new discipline, the comradely discipline of the toilers, their firm ties with the proletariat, their rallying around the proletariat, this new discipline, the new basis of social ties, which is replacing the feudal discipline of the medieval ages, the discipline of starvation, the discipline of "free" wage slavery under capitalism.

In order to abolish the classes a period of the dictatorship of one class is necessary, namely, of the oppressed class which is capable not only of overthrowing the exploiters, not only of ruthlessly suppressing their resistance, but also of breaking with the entire bourgeois democratic ideology, with all the philistine phrases about freedom and equality in general (in fact, as Marx has long ago pointed out, these phrases mean the "freedom and equality" of the *commodity owners,* the "freedom and equality" of *the capitalist* and the worker).

Furthermore, of the oppressed classes, only that class is capable of abolishing the classes by its dictatorship that has been trained, united, educated and hardened by decades of strikes and political struggle against capital – only that class that has acquired the entire urban, industrial, big capitalist culture and is determined and able to defend, maintain and develop further all its acquisitions, to make them accessible to the entire people, to all the toilers – only that class that is able to bear all the difficulties, trials, misfortunes, great sacrifices that history inevitably imposes upon those who break with the past and courageously pave for themselves the way to a new future – only that class whose best people are full of hatred and contempt for all that is philistine, for the qualities which flourish among the petty bourgeoisie, the petty employees and the "intellectuals" – only that class that has become steeled in the "school of labor" and whose efficiency commands the respect of every toiler and every honest man.

V. I. Lenin, *Collected Works,* Russian edition, Vol. XXIV, pp. 314-16.

3. The Revolutionary-Democratic Dictatorship of the Proletariat and the Peasantry as a Stage on the Way to the Dictatorship of the Proletariat[*]

One of the objections raised to the slogan "the revolutionary-democratic dictatorship of the proletariat and the peasantry" is that dictatorship presupposes a "united will" (*Iskra,* No. 95), and that there can be no united will between the proletariat and the petty bourgeoisie. This objection is fallacious, for it is based on an abstract "metaphysical" interpretation of the term "united will." Will may be united in one respect and not united in another. The absence of unity on questions of socialism and the struggle for socialism does not prevent unity of will on questions of democracy and the struggle for a republic. To forget this would be tantamount to forgetting the logical and historical difference between a democratic revolution and a socialist revolution. To forget this would mean forgetting the *national* character of the democratic revolution: if it is "national" it means that there *must* be "unity of will" precisely in so far as this revolution satisfies the national needs and requirements. Beyond the boundaries of democracy there can be no unity of will between the proletariat and the peasant bourgeoisie. Class struggle between them is inevitable; but on the basis of a democratic republic this struggle will be the most far-reaching and extensive struggle of the people for *socialism.* Like everything else in the world, the revolutionary-democratic dictatorship of the proletariat and the

---

[*] The question of the difference between the revolutionary-democratic dictatorship of the proletariat and the peasantry on the one hand and the dictatorship of the proletariat on the other is dealt with in *Theory of the Proletarian Revolution,* uniform with this volume. – *Ed.*

peasantry has a past and a future. Its past is autocracy, serfdom, monarchy and privileges. In the struggle against this past, in the struggle against counter-revolution, a "united will" of the proletariat and the peasantry is possible, for there is unity of interests.

Its future is the struggle against private property, the struggle of the wage worker against his master, the struggle for socialism. In this case, unity of will is impossible.[*] Here our path lies not from autocracy to a republic, but from a petty-bourgeois democratic re-public to socialism.

Of course, in concrete historical circumstances, the elements of the past become interwoven with those of the future, the two paths get mixed. Wage labor and its struggle against private property exist under autocracy as well, they originate even under serfdom. But this does not prevent us from drawing a logical and historical line of demarcation between the important stages of development. Surely we all draw the distinction between bourgeois revolution and socialist revolution, we all absolutely insist on the necessity of drawing a strict line between them; but can it be denied that in history certain particular elements of both revolutions become interwoven? Have there not been a number of socialist movements and attempts at establishing socialism in the period of democratic revolutions in Europe? And will not the future socialist revolution in Europe still have to do a great deal that has been left undone in the field of democracy?

A Social-Democrat must never, even for an instant, forget that the proletarian class struggle for socialism against the most demo-cratic and republican bourgeoisie and petty bourgeoisie is inevita-ble. This is beyond doubt. From this logically follows the absolute necessity of a separate, independent and strictly class party of So-cial-Democracy. From this logically follows the provisional charac-ter of our tactics to "strike together" with the bourgeoisie and the duty to carefully watch "our ally, as if he were an enemy," etc. All this is also beyond doubt. But it would be ridiculous and reactionary to deduce from this that we must forget, ignore or neglect those tasks which, although transient and temporary, are vital at the pre-

---

[*] The development of capitalism, which is more extensive and rapid under conditions of freedom, will inevitably put a speedy end to the unity of will; the sooner the counter-revolution and reaction are crushed, the speedier will the unity of will come to an end.

sent time. The struggle against autocracy is a temporary and transient task of the Socialists, but to ignore or neglect this task would be tantamount to betraying socialism and rendering a service to reaction. Certainly, the revolutionary-democratic dictatorship of the proletariat and the peasantry is only a transient, provisional task of the Socialists, but to ignore this task in the period of a democratic revolution would be simply reactionary.

Concrete political tasks must be presented in concrete circumstances. All things are relative, all things flow and are subject to change. The program of the German Social-Democratic Party does not contain the demand for a republic. In Germany the situation is such that this question can in practice hardly be separated from the question of socialism (although even as regards Germany, Engels in his comments on the draft of the Erfurt Program of 1891 uttered a warning against belittling the importance of a republic and of the struggle for a republic).* Russian Social-Democracy never raised the question of eliminating the demand for a republic from its program or agitation, for in our country there can be no indissoluble connection between the question of a republic and the question of socialism. It was quite natural for a German Social-Democrat of 1898 not to put the question of the republic in the forefront, and this evoked neither surprise nor condemnation. But a German Social-Democrat who in 1848 left the question of the republic in the shade would have been a downright traitor to the revolution. There is no such thing as abstract truth. Truth is always concrete.

The time will come when the struggle against Russian autocracy will be over, when the period of democratic revolution in Russia will also be over, and then it will be ridiculous to talk about "unity of will" of the proletariat and the peasantry, about a democratic dictatorship, etc. When that time comes we shall take up the question of the socialist dictatorship of the proletariat and *deal* with it at greater length. But at present the party of the advanced class cannot

---

* The Erfurt Program of the German Social-Democratic Party was adopted at the Erfurt Party Congress held October 14-20, 1891, and replaced the old program adopted at the Gotha Congress held June 22-27, 1875. The editor of the Erfurt Program was Kautsky, who wrote the well known theoretical preamble to it. Engels criticized the draft program in a letter addressed to Kautsky on June 29, 1891, the publication of which was, however, withheld until 1901. – *Ed.*

help striving in a most energetic manner for a decisive victory of the democratic revolution over tsarism. And a decisive victory is nothing else than the revolutionary-democratic dictatorship of the proletariat and the peasantry.

V. I. Lenin, "The 'Revolutionary Communes' and the Revolutionary-Democratic Dictatorship of the Proletariat and the Peasantry," *Selected Works,* Vol. III, pp. 98-101.

III. THE DICTATORSHIP OF THE PROLETARIAT AS A NEW TYPE OF STATE; THE SOVIETS AS A STATE FORM OF THE DICTATORSHIP OF THE PROLETARIAT

1. The Main Features of the Dictatorship of the Proletariat as the State of a New Type, as the Proletarian and Soviet Democracy

A. Stalin on the Dictatorship of the Proletariat as the State of a New Type and on the Soviets as the State Form of the Dictatorship of the Proletariat

...From the foregoing, it is quite obvious that the dictatorship of the proletariat is not a mere change of personalities in the government, a change of "cabinet," etc., leaving inviolate the old order of things economically as well as politically. The Mensheviks and opportunists of all countries, who fear dictatorship like the plague, and who, in their trepidation, palm off the concept "conquest of power" for the concept "dictatorship of the proletariat," habitually reduce the meaning of "conquest of power" to a change of "cabinet," or to a new ministry composed of people like Scheidemann and Noske, MacDonald and Henderson taking over the helm of the state. There is hardly any need to explain that these and similar cabinet changes have nothing in common with the dictatorship of the proletariat or with the conquest of real power by a real proletariat. With the MacDonalds and Scheidemanns in power, and the old bourgeois *order of* things allowed to remain, their governments, so to speak, cannot be anything but an apparatus serving the bourgeoisie, a screen to hide the sores of imperialism, a weapon in the hands of the bourgeoisie against the revolutionary movement of the oppressed and exploited masses. Capital needs such governments to screen it, when it finds it inconvenient, unprofitable or difficult to oppress and exploit the masses without the aid of such a blind. Of course the appearance of such governments is a symptom that "all is not quiet on Shipka Hill"[*] (*i.e.,* among the capitalists). Nevertheless, govern-

---

[*] A Russian saying carried over from the Russo-Turkish War of 1877. Severe fighting was taking place at Shipka Hill in which the Russians suffered severe losses and the hill was strewn with killed soldiers when the engagement ended; but Russian Headquarters in their *communiqué* reported: "All quiet on Shipka Hill." – *Ed.*

ments of this complexion necessarily remain camouflaged capitalist governments. The government of a MacDonald or a Scheidemann is as far removed from the conquest of power by the proletariat as the earth from the sky. The dictatorship of the proletariat is not a mere change of government, but a new state, with new organs of power, both central and local; it is the proletarian state which has arisen on the ruins of the old state, the state of the bourgeoisie.

The dictatorship of the proletariat does not arise on the basis of the bourgeois order; it arises while this order is being torn down, after the overthrow of the bourgeoisie, in the process of the expropriation of the landlords and capitalists, during the process of socialization of the principal instruments and means of production, in the process of violent proletarian revolution. The dictatorship of the proletariat is a revolutionary power based on violence against the bourgeoisie.

The state is an instrument in the hands of the ruling class for suppressing the resistance of its class enemies. *In this respect* the dictatorship of the proletariat in no way differs, in essence, from the dictatorship of any other class, for the proletarian state is an instrument for the suppression of the bourgeoisie. Nevertheless, there is an *essential* difference between the two, which is, that all class states that have existed heretofore have been dictatorships of an exploiting minority over the exploited majority, whereas the dictatorship of the proletariat is the dictatorship of the exploited majority over an exploiting minority.

To put it briefly: *the dictatorship of the proletariat is the domination of the proletariat over the bourgeoisie, untrammeled by law and based on violence and enjoying the sympathy and support of the toiling and exploited masses. (Cf. Lenin, The State and Revolution.)*

From this two fundamental deductions may be drawn.

First deduction: The dictatorship of the proletariat cannot be "complete" democracy, a democracy for *all,* for rich and poor alike; the dictatorship of the proletariat "must be a state that is democratic *in a new way – for* the proletariat and the poor in general – and dictatorial in *a new way – against* the bourgeoisie... (*The State and Revolution,* my italics – *J. S.*). The talk of Kautsky and Co. about universal equality, about "pure" democracy, about "perfect" democracy and the like, are but bourgeois screens to conceal the indubitable fact that equality between exploited and exploiters is impossible. The theory of "pure" democracy is the theory of the upper stratum of the working class which is tamed and fed by the imperialist plunderers. It was invented to hide the sores of capitalism, to camouflage imperialism and lend it moral strength in its struggle against the exploited masses. Under the capitalist system there is no true "freedom" for the exploited, nor can there be, if for no other reason than that the buildings, printing plants, paper supplies, etc., indispensable for the actual enjoyment of this "freedom," are the privilege of the exploiters. Under the capitalist system the exploited masses do not, nor can they really participate in the administration of the country, if for no other reason than that even with the most democratic system under capitalism, the governments are set up not by the people, but by the Rothschilds and Stinneses, the Morgans and Rockefellers. Democracy under the capitalist system is *capitalist* democracy, the democracy of an exploiting minority based upon the restriction of the rights of the exploited majority and directed against this majority. Only under the dictatorship of the proletariat is real "freedom" for the exploited and real participation in the administration of the country by the proletarians and peasants possible. Under the dictatorship of the proletariat, democracy is *proletarian* democracy – the democracy of the exploited majority based upon the restriction of the rights of the exploiting minority and directed against this minority.

Second deduction: the dictatorship of the proletariat cannot come about as a result of the peaceful development of bourgeois society and of bourgeois democracy; it can come only as the result of the destruction of the bourgeois state machine, of the bourgeois army, of the bourgeois civil administration and of the bourgeois police.

In their preface to *The Civil War in France,* Marx and Engels wrote:

> The working class cannot simply take possession of the ready-made state machine and use it for its own purposes.

In his letter to Kugelmann (April 12, 1871), Marx wrote that the task of the proletarian revolution must

> be no longer, as before, to transfer the bureaucratic-military machine from one hand to another, but to *smash* it, and that is essential for every real people's revolution on the Continent.

Marx's qualifying phrase about the Continent gave to the opportunists and Mensheviks of all countries a pretext to cry aloud that Marx admitted the possibility of the peaceful evolution of bourgeois democracy into a proletarian democracy at least in certain countries which do not come within the European continental system (England, United States). Marx did in fact concede that possibility, and he had good grounds for doing so in regard to the England and the United States of the seventies of the last century, when monopoly capitalism and imperialism did not yet exist and when these countries, owing to the special conditions of their development, had as yet no developed militarism or bureaucracy. That is how matters stood before developed imperialism made its appearance. But later, after a lapse of thirty to forty years, when the state of affairs in these countries had undergone a radical change, when imperialism had developed and had embraced all capitalist countries without exception, when militarism and bureaucracy appeared in England and the United States also, when the special conditions of peaceful development in England and the United States had disappeared – then the qualification in regard to these countries could no longer apply.

Lenin said:

> Today, in 1917, in the epoch of the first great imperialist war, Marx's exception is no longer valid. Both England and America, the greatest and last representatives of Anglo-Saxon "liberty" in the whole world, in the sense that militarism and bureaucracy are absent, have today plunged headlong into the all-European, filthy, bloody morass of military bureaucratic institutions to which everything is subordinated and which trample everything underfoot. Today, both in England and America, the essential thing for every real people's revolution is the smashing, the destruction of the "ready-made" state machinery (brought in those countries, between 1914 and 1917, to general "European" imperialist perfection. (*The State and Revolution.*)

In other words, the law of violent proletarian revolution, the law of destruction of the machinery of the bourgeois state as a condition precedent for such revolution is an inevitable law of the revolutionary movement in the imperialist countries of the world.

Of course, in the remote future, if the proletariat is victorious in the most important capitalist countries and if the present capitalist encirclement gives way to a socialist encirclement, a "peaceful" course of development is quite possible for some of the capitalist countries whose capitalists, in view of the "unfavorable" international situation, will consider it advisable "voluntarily" to make substantial concessions to the proletariat. But this supposition deals only with the remote and possible future; it has no bearing whatever on the immediate future.

Lenin is therefore right in saying:

> The proletarian revolution is impossible without the forcible destruction of the bourgeois state machine and the substitution for it of a *new one*. (*The Proletarian Revolution and Renegade Kautsky*, p. 21.)

...The victory of the dictatorship of the proletariat signifies the suppression of the bourgeoisie, the break-up of the bourgeois state machine and the replacement of bourgeois democracy by proletarian democracy. That is clear. But what organizations are to be employed in order to carry out this colossal work? There can hardly be any doubt that the old forms of organization of the proletariat which grew up with bourgeois parliamentarism as their base, are not equal to this task. What are the new forms of organization of the proletariat that can serve as the grave-digger of the bourgeois state machine, that are capable not only of breaking this machine, not only of replacing bourgeois democracy by proletarian democracy, but also of serving as the foundation of the state power of the proletariat?

This new form of organization of the proletariat is the soviets.

In what lies the strength of the soviets as compared with the old forms of organization?

In that the soviets are the most *all-embracing* mass organizations of the proletariat, for they and they alone embrace all workers without exception.

In that the soviets are the *only* mass organizations that take in all the oppressed and exploited workers and peasants, soldiers and sailors, and for this reason the political leadership of the mass struggle by the vanguard, by the proletariat, can be most easily and most completely exercised through them.

In that the soviets are the *most powerful organs* of the revolutionary mass struggle, of mass political demonstrations and of mass uprising; they are organs capable of breaking the omnipotence of finance capital and its political accessories.

In that the soviets are the *direct* organizations of the masses themselves, *i.e.,* they are *the most democratic,* and therefore the most authoritative organizations of the masses, that provide them with the maximum facilities for participating in the building up of the new state and its administration; they develop to their fullest extent the revolutionary energy, the initiative and the creative faculties of the masses in the struggle for the destruction of the old system, in the struggle for a new, proletarian system.

The Soviet power is the unification and the crystallization of the local soviets into one general state organization, into a state organization of the proletariat which is both the vanguard of the oppressed and exploited masses and the ruling class – it is their unification into the republic of soviets.

The essence of the Soviet power is the fact that the most pronounced mass and revolutionary organizations of precisely those classes that were oppressed by the capitalists and landlords now constitute the *"permanent* and *sole* foundation of all state power, of the entire state apparatus"; that "precisely those masses which in the most democratic bourgeois republics" enjoy equal rights according to the letter of the law, but "in fact by a thousand tricks and machinations were prevented from participating in political life and from exercising their democratic rights and liberties, are now *constantly,* imperatively drawn into participation, and, moreover, into *decisive* participation in the democratic administration of the state." (V. I. Lenin, *Collected Works,* Russian edition, Vol. XXIV, p. 13.)

For this reason the Soviet power is a *new form* of state organization, different in principle from the old bourgeois-democratic and parliamentary form – a *new type* of state adapted, not to the task of exploiting and oppressing the toiling masses but to the task of completely emancipating them from all oppression and exploitation, to the tasks facing the dictatorship of the proletariat.

Lenin rightly says that with the appearance of the Soviet power "the epoch of bourgeois-democratic parliamentarism has come to an end and a new chapter in world history has commenced: the epoch of proletarian dictatorship."

What are the main characteristics of the Soviet power?

They are that the Soviet power has a most pronounced mass character and is the most democratic of all state organizations possible while classes continue to exist; for, being the arena of the bond and cooperation of the workers and exploited peasants in their struggle against the exploiters, and basing itself in its work on this bond and cooperation, the Soviet power by this very fact represents the rule of the majority of the population over the minority, it is the state of that majority, the expression of its dictatorship.

That the Soviet power is the most international of all state organizations in class society, for, by extirpating every kind of national oppression and basing itself on the cooperation of the toiling masses of the various nationalities it facilitates the amalgamation of these masses into a single union of states.

That the Soviet power by its very structure facilitates the leadership of the oppressed and exploited masses by the vanguard of these masses, i.e., the proletariat – the most compact and most class conscious nucleus of the soviets.

> The experience of all revolutions and of all movements of the oppressed classes, the experience of the world socialist movement teaches us (says Lenin) that only the proletariat is able to unite the scattered, backward strata of the toiling and exploited population and to lead them. (*Ibid.,* p. 14.)

The structure of the Soviet power facilitates the practical application of the lessons to be drawn from this experience.

That the Soviet power, by combining the legislative and executive functions in a single state body and replacing territorial electoral divisions by units of production, *i.e.,* factories and workshops, thereby directly connects the workers and the laboring masses in general with the apparatus of state administration and teaches them how to administer the country.

That only the Soviet power is capable of releasing the army from its position of subordination to bourgeois command and of converting it from an instrument of oppression of the people, which it is under the bourgeois order, into an instrument for the liberation of the people from the yoke of the bourgeoisie, both native and foreign.

That "only the Soviet state organization can definitely destroy at one blow the old, *i.e.,* the bourgeois-bureaucratic and judicial apparatus." (*Ibid.*)

That the Soviet form of state alone, by drawing the mass organizations of the toilers and of the exploited into constant and unconditional participation in the administration of the state, is capable of preparing the ground for the dying out of the state which is one of the basic elements of the future stateless communist society.

The republic of soviets is thus the political form, so long sought and finally found, within the framework of which the economic emancipation of the proletariat and the complete victory of socialism is to be accomplished.

The Paris Commune was the embryo of this form; the Soviet power is its development and culmination.

That is why Lenin says that:

> The Republic of soviets of workers', soldiers' and peasants' deputies is not only the form of a higher type of democratic institution... but is also the *only form* capable of insuring the least painful transition to socialism. (*Collected Works,* Russian edition, Vol. XXII, p. 131.)

Joseph Stalin, *Leninism,* Vol. I, pp. 44-51.

B. The Dictatorship of the Proletariat – the State of a New Type

Thus, the Dictatorship of the Proletariat is a "political transition period"; it is clear that also *the state of this period* is a transition from the state to no state, *i.e.,* "no longer a state in the proper sense of the word." Marx and Engels therefore do not in any way contradict each other on this point.

But further on Marx speaks of "the future state of communist society"!! Thus, even in "communist society" the state will exist!! Is there not a contradiction in this?

The state is needed by the bourgeoisie	No: I – in capitalist society, a state in the proper sense of the word.
The state is needed by the proletariat	II – the transition (dictatorship of the proletariat): a state of the transitional type (not a state in the proper sense of the word).

The state is not needed, it withers away	III – communist society: the *withering away* of the state.
Complete consistency and clarity!!	In other words:
I – Democracy only for the rich and for a small layer of the proletariat. (It is not for the poor man!)	I – Democracy only by way of exception and never complete. ...
П – Democracy for the poor, for 9/10 of the population, the crushing of the resistance of the rich by force.	II – Democracy almost complete, limited only by the *crushing* of the resistance of the bourgeoisie
III – Democracy complete, becoming a habit and for that reason dying out, giving place to the principle: "from each according to his abilities, to each according to his needs."	III – Democracy, really complete, becoming a habit and *for that reason* dying out.... Complete democracy equals no democracy. This is not a paradox but the truth!

See p. 19, marginal note.

V. I. Lenin, *Miscellany,* Volume XIV, pp. 265-266. (From Lenin's notes in connection with the work on the state which he was preparing. The notes were entered in a special note-book in January and February, 1917.) – *Ed.*

C. The Paris Commune as the First Historical Experience of the New Type of State

From the outset the Commune was compelled to recognize that, the working class, once come to power, could not manage with the old state machine; that in order not to lose again its newly-won supremacy, this working class must, on the one hand, do away with all the old repressive machinery previously used against itself, and, on the other, safeguard itself against its own deputies and officials, by declaring them all, without exception, subject to recall at any moment. What had been the characteristic attribute of the old state? Society had created its own organs to look after its common interests, originally through the simple division of labor. But these organs, at whose head was the State power, had in the course of time, in pursuance of their own special interests, transformed themselves from the servants of society into the masters of society, as can be seen, for example, not only in the hereditary monarchy, but equally also in the democratic republic. Nowhere do "politicians" form a more separate powerful section of the nation than in North America. There, each of the two great parties which alternately succeed each other in power is itself in turn controlled by people who make a business of politics, who speculate on seats in the legislative assemblies of the Union as well as of the separate states, or who make a living by carrying on agitation for their party and on its victory are rewarded with positions. It is well known that the Americans have been striving for thirty years to shake off this yoke, which has become intolerable, and in spite of all they can do they continue to sink ever deeper in this swamp of corruption. It is precisely in America that we see best how there takes place this process of the State power making itself independent in relation to society, whose mere instrument it was originally intended to be. Here there exists no dynasty, no nobility, no standing army, beyond the few men keeping watch on the Indians; no bureaucracy with permanent posts or the right to pensions. And nevertheless we find here two great gangs of political speculators, who alternately take possession of the State power, and exploit it by the most corrupt means and for the most corrupt ends – and the nation is powerless against these two great cartels of politicians, who are ostensibly its servants, but in reality exploit and plunder it.

Against this transformation of the State and the organs of the State from the servants of society into masters of society – an inevitable transformation in all previous states – the Commune made use of two infallible expedients. In the first place, it filled all posts – administrative, judicial and educational – by election on the basis of universal suffrage of all concerned, with the right of the same electors to recall their delegate at any time. And in the second place, all officials, high or low, were paid only the wages received by other workers. The highest salary paid by the Commune to anyone was 6,000 francs. In this way an effective barrier to place-hunting and careerism was set up, even apart from the superabundance of mandates to delegates to representative bodies which were also added in proportion.

The shattering of the former state power and its replacement by a new and really democratic state is described in detail in the third section of *The Civil War:* But it was necessary to dwell briefly here once more on some of its features, because in Germany particularly the superstitious belief in the state has been carried over from philosophy into the general consciousness of the bourgeoisie and even of many workers. According to the philosophical notion the state is the "realization of the idea" or, the Kingdom of God on earth translated into philosophical terms; the sphere in which eternal truth and justice is or should be realized. And from this follows a superstitious reverence of the state and everything connected with it, which takes root the more readily as people from their childhood are accustomed to imagine that the affairs and interests common to the whole of society could not be looked after otherwise than as they have been looked after in the past, that is through the state and its well-paid officials. And people think they are taking quite an extraordinarily bold step forward when they rid themselves of belief in a hereditary monarchy and swear by the democratic republic. In reality, however, the State is nothing more than a machine for the oppression of one class by another, and indeed in the democratic republic no less than in the monarchy; and at best an evil inherited by the proletariat, after its victorious struggle for class supremacy, whose worst sides the proletariat, just like the Commune, cannot avoid having to lop off at the earliest possible moment, until such time as a new generation, reared in new and free social conditions, will be able to throw the entire lumber of the state on the scrap heap.

Of late the Social-Democratic philistine[*] has once more been filled with wholesome terror at the words: Dictatorship of the Proletariat. Well and good, gentlemen, do you want to know what this dictatorship looks like? Look at the Paris Commune. That was the Dictatorship of the Proletariat.

Frederick Engels, Introduction to *The Civil War in France,* by Karl Marx, London and New York, 1933.

D. The Dictatorship of the Proletariat as the Proletarian

---

[*] In all editions published before 1932 the text had the words, "the German philistine." This was a falsification. Engels' manuscript in the possession of the Marx-Engels-Lenin Institute in Moscow has the words "Social-Democratic philistine." The word "Social-Democratic" was afterwards crossed out (not by Engels) and the word "German" was inserted in an unknown handwriting. – *Ed.*

1. The bourgeois republic, even the most democratic, sanctified by the slogans of the national or non-class will of the people, has inevitably proved in fact to be – owing to the private ownership of the land and other means of production – the dictatorship of the bourgeoisie, a machine for the exploitation and suppression of the overwhelming majority of the toilers by a handful of capitalists. In contrast to this, proletarian or Soviet democracy has transformed the mass organizations of precisely the classes oppressed by capitalism, the proletarians and poor peasants (semi-proletarians), *i.e.,* the enormous majority of the population, into the sole and permanent basis of the entire state apparatus, local and central, from top to bottom. In this way, the Soviet government introduced (and, incidentally, in a much wider form than anywhere else) local and regional self-government, without any official authorities appointed from above. The task of the Party is to work untiringly for the complete and actual realization of this highest type of democracy, which, in order that it may function properly, requires a steady raising of the level of culture, organization and activity of the masses.

2. In contrast to bourgeois democracy, which conceals the class nature of its state, the Soviet power openly recognizes that every state must inevitably be a class state until the division of society into classes and along with it all state power have completely disappeared. By its very nature, the object of the Soviet state is to crush the resistance of the exploiters; and the Soviet constitution, proceeding from the standpoint that all freedom is a deception if it runs counter to the emancipation of labor from the yoke of capital, does not hesitate to deprive the exploiters of political rights. The task of the Party of the proletariat is, while steadily pursuing the policy of suppressing the resistance of the exploiters and combating ideologically the deep-rooted prejudices concerning the absolute nature of bourgeois rights and liberties, to explain that deprivation of political rights and restriction of liberty are necessary only as temporary measures to fight any attempt of the exploiters to defend or restore their privileges. To the extent that the objective possibility of exploitation of man by man disappears, the necessity for such temporary measures will also disappear, and the Party will strive to diminish these measures and finally to abolish them.

3. Bourgeois democracy has confined itself to the formal extension of political rights and liberties, such as the right of assembly,

right of association, and freedom of the press, to all citizens alike. In reality, however, administrative practice, and, above all, the economic enslavement of the toilers, have always made it impossible for the toilers to enjoy these rights and liberties to any real extent under bourgeois democracy.

Proletarian democracy, on the contrary, instead of formally proclaiming rights and liberties, actually grants them, primarily and mainly to those classes of the population which have been oppressed by capitalism, namely the proletariat and the peasantry. For this purpose the Soviet government expropriates from the bourgeoisie buildings, printing plants, stocks of paper, etc., and places them at the complete disposal of the workers and their organizations.

The task of the Communist Party of the Soviet Union is to draw broader and broader masses of the toiling population into using democratic rights and liberties and to extend the material possibilities for this.

4. For centuries bourgeois democracy has been proclaiming equality irrespective of sex, religion, race and nationality, but capitalism never allowed this equality to be realized in practice anywhere; and during its imperialist stage it has caused a very strong increase in racial and national oppression. It is only because it is the government of the toilers that the Soviet government was able for the first time in history to introduce this equality of rights completely and in all spheres of life, including the absolute elimination of the last traces of inequality of women in the sphere of marriage and family rights in general. The task of the Party at the present moment is mainly to carry on ideological and educational work for the purpose of finally stamping out all traces of former inequality or prejudices, especially among the backward strata of the proletariat and the peasantry.

Not confining itself to the formal equality of women, the Party strives to free women from the material burden of obsolete housekeeping by substituting for it house-communes, public dining halls, central laundries, crèches, etc.

5. While securing for the toiling masses incomparably greater opportunities than those enjoyed under bourgeois democracy and parliamentary government to elect and recall deputies in a manner easiest and most accessible to the workers and peasants, the Soviet government at the same time abolishes the negative aspect of parliamentary government, especially the separation of the legislature

from the executive, the isolation of the representative institution from the masses, etc.

The Soviet government draws the state apparatus closer to the masses also by the fact that the electoral constituency and the basic unit of the state is no longer a territorial district, but an industrial unit (works, factory).

The task of the Party is, while pursuing all its work in this direction, to bring the organs of power still closer to the masses of the toilers on the basis of an ever stricter and fuller application of democracy by the masses in practice, especially by making officials responsible and accountable for their actions.

6. Whereas bourgeois democracy, in spite of its declarations, has converted its army into a weapon of the propertied classes, separating it from the toiling masses and opposing it to them, and has made it difficult or even impossible for soldiers to exercise their political rights, the Soviet state merges the workers and soldiers in its organs, the Soviets, on the basis of complete equality of rights and identity of interests. The task of the Party is to maintain and develop this solidarity of workers and soldiers in the Soviets, to strengthen the indissoluble ties between the armed forces and the organizations of the proletariat and the semi-proletariat.

7. The leading role of the industrial urban proletariat played throughout the revolution as the section of the toiling masses which is most concentrated, united and enlightened and most hardened in the struggle manifested itself in the rise of the Soviets as well as in the whole course of their evolution into organs of power. Our Soviet constitution reflects this by preserving certain advantages for the industrial proletariat as compared with the more scattered petty-bourgeois masses in the rural districts.

While explaining the temporary nature of these advantages, which are historically bound up with the difficulties attending the organization of the rural districts on socialist lines, the Communist Party of the Soviet Union must strive to secure the steady and systematic utilization of this position by the industrial workers in order, in contrast to the narrow craft and narrow trade interests fostered by capitalism among the workers, to unite more closely the advanced workers with the more backward and scattered masses of the rural proletarians and semi-proletarians and also the middle peasantry.*

----

* In 1935 the Communist Party and the Soviet government, upon the

8. It was only thanks to the Soviet organization of the state that the proletarian revolution was able immediately to smash and radically destroy the old bourgeois bureaucratic and juridical state apparatus. However, the inadequate cultural level of the broad masses, the lack of necessary experience in administrative affairs among the workers promoted by the masses to occupy responsible posts, the necessity hurriedly and under difficult conditions to enlist specialists of the old school and to divert the most educated stratum of the urban workers to military work have brought about a partial revival of bureaucracy in the Soviet system.

While conducting a most determined struggle against bureaucracy, the Communist Party of the Soviet Union advocates the following measures for the complete elimination of this evil:

1. The obligatory participation of every member of the Soviet in definite work connected with the administration of the state.

2. Consecutive rotation in this work so that every member is able to acquire experience in all branches of administration.

3. The entire toiling population to be gradually drawn into the work of state administration.

---

initiative of Stalin, decided to introduce certain changes in the Soviet constitution. To-day, when, thanks to the rapid growth of the productive forces of the socialist country, the working class of the U.S.S.R. has increased in numbers several times, when in the countryside collectivization has been victorious, when the toiling peasantry has decidedly taken the road of socialism, when the kulak has been finally crushed, and when the influence of the party has grown to an enormous degree, there is no longer any need for the proletariat to have special advantages in the election rights. Its influence and leading role is to-day assured even without these advantages.

The Seventh All-Union Congress of the Soviets has therefore decided to substitute equal, direct and secret elections for the unequal, indirect and open elections. This change in the election system towards a still wider democracy is far from signifying a weakening of the leading role of the proletariat; it is, on the contrary, a sign of the growth and might of the Soviet Union, of the further strengthening of the dictatorship of the proletariat. The new election system will strengthen still further the firm and direct contact between the state apparatus of the proletarian dictatorship and the toiling masses, and thus guarantee an even greater development of Soviet democracy. (Cf. *The New Soviet Constitution,* Proposed Draft.) – *Ed.*

The complete and extensive application of all these measures, which represent a further step along the path taken by the Paris Commune, and the simplification of the functions of administration, together with the raising of the cultural level of the toilers, will lead towards the abolition of state power.

Program and Rules of the Communist Party of the Soviet Union.

E. The Main Features of the Soviets as the State Form of the Dictatorship of the Proletariat

The Soviets are a new state apparatus, which, in the first place, provides an armed force of workers and peasants; and this force is not divorced from the people, as was the old standing army, but is fused with the people in the closest possible fashion. From a military point of view, this force is incomparably more powerful than previous forces; from the point of view of the revolution it cannot be replaced by anything else. Secondly, this apparatus provides a bond with the masses, with the majority of the people, so intimate, so indissoluble, so readily controllable and renewable, that there was nothing remotely like it in the previous state apparatus. Thirdly, this apparatus, by virtue of the fact that it is elected and is subject to recall at the will of the people without any bureaucratic formalities, is far more democratic than any previous apparatus. Fourthly, it provides a close contact with the most diverse occupations, thus facilitating the adoption of the most varied and most radical reforms without a bureaucracy. Fifthly, it provides a form of organization of the vanguard, *i.e.*, of the most class-conscious, most energetic and most progressive section of the oppressed classes, the workers and peasants, and thus constitutes an apparatus with the help of which the vanguard of the oppressed classes can elevate, educate and lead *the gigantic masses* of these classes which hitherto have stood remote from political life and from history. Sixthly, it provides the possibility of combining the advantages of parliamentarism with the advantages of immediate and direct democracy, *i.e.,* of uniting in the persons of elected representatives of the people both legislative and *executive* functions. Compared with bourgeois parliamentarism, this represents an advance in the development of democracy which is of historical and world-wide significance.

...If the creative impulse of the revolutionary classes of the people had not engendered the Soviets, the proletarian revolution in

Russia would have been a hopeless cause. For the proletariat could certainly not have retained power with the old state apparatus, while it is impossible to create a new apparatus immediately.

V. I. Lenin, "Can the Bolsheviks Retain State Power?" *Selected Works,* Vol. VI, pp. 263-264.

The consolidation and development of the Soviet power as a form of the dictatorship of the proletariat and the poor peasantry (semi-proletarians) was tested by experience, that had sprung up in the course of the mass movement and the revolutionary struggle.

This consolidation and development should consist in the realization (on a broader, general and planned scale) of the following tasks imposed by history upon this form of state power, this new type of state.

1. To unite and organize the toiling and exploited masses oppressed by capitalism and these only, *i.e.,* only workers and poor peasants, semi-proletarians, while automatically excluding the exploiting classes and the rich representatives of the petty-bourgeoisie;

2. To unite the more active, class-conscious section of the oppressed classes, their vanguard, which must train the entire toiling population independently to take part in the management of the state, not theoretically but practically.

3. To abolish parliamentarism (the separation of legislative from executive work); to combine legislative and executive state work. To amalgamate administration and legislation.

4. To establish a closer connection between the masses and the entire apparatus of the state power and state administration than prevailed under the old forms of democracy.

5. To create an armed force of workers and peasants least isolated from the people (soviets – armed workers and peasants). The organization of the arming of the whole people is one of the first steps towards the complete realization of the arming of the whole people.

6. To achieve more complete democracy by reducing formalities and offering greater facilities for election and recall.

7. To establish close (and direct) connection with the trades and the industrial economic units (elections by factories, by local peasant and handicraft regions). This close connection offers the possibility of effecting deep socialist changes.

8. (Partly, if not entirely, included in the previous clauses) – the possibility of removing bureaucracy, of managing without it, making a start with the realization of this possibility.

9. In questions of democracy, instead of formal recognition of the formal equality of the bourgeoisie and the proletariat, of the poor and the rich, to lay the greatest stress on giving practical effect to the enjoyment of freedom (democracy) by the toiling and exploited masses of the population.

10. To further the development of the soviet organization of the state so that each member of the soviet along with his participation in the meetings of the soviet undertakes constant work of state administration, and then gradually to get the whole population to participate in soviet organizations (provided they submit to the toilers' organizations) as well as to undertake certain duties of state administration.

V. I. Lenin, *Collected Works,* Russian edition, Vol. XXII, pp. 371-72.

2. The Proletarian Nature of the Soviet State and the Substance of the Slogan Workers' and Peasants' Government

Our state must not be confused, *i.e.,* identified, with our government. Our state is the organization of the *class* of proletarians as a state power, the purpose of which is to crush the resistance of the exploiters, organize socialist economy, abolish classes, and so on. Our government, however, is the upper part of that state organization, the guiding part. The government may make mistakes, it may commit blunders that may involve the danger of a temporary collapse of the dictatorship of the proletariat; but that would not mean that the proletarian dictatorship as the principle of the structure of the state in the transition period is wrong or mistaken. It would only mean that the leadership is bad, that the policy of the leadership, the policy of the government, does not correspond with the dictatorship of the proletariat, that that policy must be changed to *correspond with* the demands of the dictatorship of the proletariat. The state and the government are alike in their class nature, but the government is narrower in scope and is not co-extensive with the state. They are organically connected with and dependent on one another, but that does not mean that they can be thrown into the same heap.

You see that the question of our state must not be confused with the question of our government, just as the question of the class of proletarians must not be confused with the question of the leadership of the proletarian class.

But still less permissible is it to confuse the question of the class nature of our state and of our government with the question of the day-to-day policy of our government. The class nature of our state and of our government is obvious – it is proletarian. The aims of our state and of our government are also obvious – they are: to crush the resistance of the exploiters, to organize socialist economy, to abolish classes, and so forth. All this is perfectly clear. What then does the question of the day-to-day policy of our government reduce itself to? It reduces itself to the question of the ways and means by which the class aims of the proletarian dictatorship may be achieved in our peasant country. The proletarian state is necessary in order to crush the resistance of the exploiters, to organize socialist economy, abolish classes and so forth. Our government, however, in addition to all this, is necessary for the purpose of indicating the *ways* and *means* (the day-to-day policy), without which the achievement of these aims would be impossible in our country where the proletariat represents the minority, where the peasantry represents the enormous majority. What are these ways and means: what do they reduce themselves to? Fundamentally, they reduce themselves to the measures that are taken towards maintaining and strengthening the *alliance* between the workers and the basic masses of the peasants, to maintaining and strengthening the leading role in that alliance of the proletariat which is in power. It need hardly be shown that without, or apart from, *such* an alliance, our government would be impotent and that it would be impossible to achieve the aims of the dictatorship of the proletariat to which I have just referred. How long will this alliance, this bond exist and how long will the Soviet government's policy of strengthening this alliance, this bond continue? Obviously, as long as classes exist and as long as a government which is the expression of class society, which is an expression of the dictatorship of the proletariat, exists. In this connection it should be borne in mind that (a) we need an alliance of the workers and the peasants, not in order to preserve the peasantry as a class, but in order to transform it and remold it in a manner corresponding to the interests of the victory of socialist construction and (b) the Soviet government's policy of strengthening that alliance is intended not to perpetuate classes, but to abolish them, to hasten the abolition of classes. Lenin, therefore, was absolutely right when he wrote:

> The supreme principle of the dictatorship is the preservation of the alliance between the proletariat and the peasantry, in order that the proletariat may retain the leading role and state power. (*Collected Works,* Russian edition, Vol. XXVI, p. 460.)

There is no need to show that it is this thesis of Lenin's and no other that is the guiding line of the day-to-day policy of the Soviet government, that the policy of the Soviet government at the present stage of development is essentially a policy of preserving and strengthening precisely such an alliance between the workers and the basic masses of the peasants. It is *in this sense,* and in this sense alone, and not in the sense of its class nature, that the Soviet government is a *workers' and peasants' government.* Not to recognize this is to deviate from the path of Leninism, to enter the path of rejecting the idea of the bond, the idea of an alliance between the proletariat and the toiling masses of the peasantry. Not to recognize this is to regard the bond as a mere maneuver, and not as a genuine revolutionary matter; is to believe that we introduced N.E.P. merely for "agitational purposes," and not for the purpose of socialist construction in conjunction with the basic masses of the peasantry. Not to recognize this is to believe that the *fundamental* interests of the basic masses of the peasantry cannot be satisfied by our revolution, that these interests are irreconcilably contradictory to the interests of the proletariat that we cannot and should not build socialism in conjunction with the basic masses of the peasantry, that Lenin's cooperative plan is unsound, and that the Mensheviks and their supporters are right and so forth. It is sufficient to put these questions to understand how hollow and worthless is the "agitational" approach to this cardinal question of the bond. That is why I said in my *Questions and Answers* that the slogan of a workers' and peasants' government was not "demagogy" and not an "agitational" maneuver, but that it was an absolutely correct and revolutionary slogan.

Briefly: the question of the class nature of the state and of the government, which determines the fundamental aims of the development of our revolution, is one thing, and the question of the day-to-day policy of the government, of the *ways* and *means* of carrying out that policy in order to achieve those aims, is another thing. These questions are, of course, interconnected. But that does not mean that they are identical, that they can be thrown into one heap.

You see that the question of the class nature of the state and of the government must not be confused with the question of the day-to-day policy of the government.

It might be said that there is a contradiction here: how can a government that is proletarian in its class nature be called a workers' and peasants' government? But the contradiction is only an apparent one. Strictly speaking it is the same sort of "contradiction" as some of our wiseacres profess to see between Lenin's two formulas regarding the dictatorship of the proletariat, the first of which states that the "dictatorship of the proletariat is the power of a single class" (*Collected Works,* Russian edition, Vol. XXIV, p. 398), while the second states that "the dictatorship of the proletariat is a *special form of class alliance* between the proletariat, the vanguard of the toilers, and the numerous non-proletarian strata of toilers (petty bourgeoisie, small owners, peasantry, intellectuals, etc." (*Collected Works,* Russian edition, Vol. XXIV, p. 311). Is there any contradiction between these two formulas? Of course not. How then is the power of a *single* class (the proletariat) achieved in a class alliance, let us say, with the basic masses of the peasantry? By the proletariat ("the vanguard of the toilers") which is in power and which is exercising leadership in this alliance. The power of a single class, the class of proletarians, exercised with the aid of an alliance between the class and the basic mass of the peasantry in the form of *state* leadership over the latter, such is the fundamental idea of these two formulas. Where is the contradiction? What is meant by the *state* leadership of the proletariat in relation to the basic mass of the peasantry? Is it the same sort of leadership that existed, for instance, in the period of the bourgeois democratic revolution when we strove for the dictatorship of the proletariat and the peasantry? No, it is not that sort of leadership. The *state* leadership of the proletariat in relation to the peasantry is leadership exercised under the dictatorship of the proletariat. The *state* leadership of the proletariat means that (a) the bourgeoisie is already overthrown; (b) the proletariat is in power; (c) the proletariat does not share power with other classes; and (d) the proletariat is building socialism and in this is leading the basic masses of the peasantry. The leadership of the proletariat in a bourgeois-democratic revolution and under the dictatorship of the proletariat and the peasantry means, however, that (a) capitalism remains as the basis; (b) the revolutionary-democratic bourgeoisie is in power, and represents the predominant force in the government; (c) the democratic bourgeoisie shares power with the proletariat; (d) the proletariat emancipates the peasantry from the influence of the bourgeois parties, leads the peasantry ideologically and politically and prepares for the struggle to overthrow capitalism. The difference, you will see, is a fundamental one.

The same must be said in regard to the question of the workers' and peasants' government. What is there contradictory in the fact that the proletarian nature of our government, and the socialist tasks that follow therefrom, not only do not prevent it from pursuing, but on the contrary compel it, necessarily compel it, to pursue a policy of maintaining and strengthening the alliance of the workers and peasants as the most important means of achieving the socialist class tasks of the proletarian dictatorship in our peasant country, and that this government is consequently called a workers' and peasants' government? Is it not obvious that Lenin was right when he carried out the slogan of a workers' and peasants' government and when he qualified our government as a workers' and peasants' government?

Generally it must be said that "the system of the dictatorship of the proletariat," with the aid of which the power of a single class, the power of the proletariat, is exercised in our country, is a rather complicated one. I know that this is not to the taste of certain comrades, they do not like it. I know that on "the principle of the least expenditure of energy" some of them would have preferred a simpler and easier system. But what can one do? Firstly, you have got to accept Leninism as it is (Leninism must not be simplified and vulgarized); secondly, history teaches us that the simplest and easiest "theories" are not always the most correct by a long way.

In your letter you complain that:

> The sin of all the comrades who deal with this question is that they either speak only of the government, or only of the state, and consequently, do not give a final answer and entirely fail to explain what relation should exist between these concepts.

I admit that certain of our leading comrades are indeed guilty of this "sin," especially if we bear in mind that certain not very diligent "readers" will not themselves make a careful study of the works of Lenin, but demand that every phrase be thoroughly masticated for them. But what can one do? Firstly, our leading comrades are too busy, too overburdened with current work and therefore cannot find time to make an exposition of Leninism point by point as one might say; secondly, something must be left for the "readers," who, after all, ought to pass from merely *perusing* the works of Lenin, to a serious *study* of Leninism. And it must be said that unless the "readers" really make a serious study of Leninism, complaints like yours and "misunderstandings" are always bound to arise.

Take, for instance, the question of our state. It is obvious that in its class nature, its program, its fundamental aims, its actions, and deeds, our state is a proletarian state, a workers' state, with certain "bureaucratic distortions," it is true. You will remember the definition given by Lenin:

> A workers' state is an abstraction. In actual fact we have a workers' state, firstly, with the peculiarity that it is not the working class population but the peasant population that is predominant in the country and that, secondly, it is a workers' state with bureaucratic distortions. (*Collected Works,* Russian edition, Vol. XXVI, p. 91.)

Only Mensheviks, Socialist-Revolutionaries and certain of our oppositionists can doubt this. Lenin repeatedly explained that our state is the state of the proletarian dictatorship and the proletarian dictatorship is the power of a single class, the power of the proletariat. All this has long been known. Nevertheless, not a few "readers" have complained, and still complain that Lenin sometimes called our state a "workers' and peasants'" state, although it is not difficult to understand that Lenin had in mind not the definition of the class nature of our state, still less the denial of the proletarian nature of that state; but that the proletarian nature of the Soviet state leads to the necessity for a bond between the proletariat and the basic masses of the peasantry and that, consequently, the policy of the Soviet government must be directed towards strengthening this bond. Take, for instance, Vol. XXII, p. 174, Vol. XXV, pp. 50, 80; Vol. XXVI, pp. 40, 67, 207, 216 and Vol. XXVII, p. 47.[*] In all these as well as in several other of his works, Lenin describes our state as being a *"workers' and peasants'"* state. But it would be strange indeed not to understand that in all such cases Lenin did not intend to describe the class nature of our state, but to define the policy of

---

[*] Russian editions. – *Ed.*

strengthening the bond that follows from the proletarian nature and socialist tasks of our state under the conditions prevailing in our peasant country. Only in this conditional and limited sense, and *only in that sense,* can one speak of a "workers' and peasants'" state, as Lenin does in the indicated passages in his works. Regarding the class nature of our state, Lenin, as I have already mentioned, gives a most precise formula, permitting of no misinterpretation, namely, a workers' state with bureaucratic distortions in a country with a predominantly peasant population.

Joseph Stalin, *Leninism,* Vol. I, pp. 324-330.

3. The Bureaucratic Distortions in the Proletarian State, the Roots of Bureaucracy and the Fight Against Bureaucracy

In conclusion I will only say a few words on the question of fighting bureaucracy which occupied so much of our time. In the summer of last year, this question was raised at the Central Committee, in August the Central Committee raised it in a circular letter to the organizations, in September it was raised at the Party Conference and finally at the December Congress of the Soviets the question was raised on a broader scale. There is no denying the existence of the bureaucratic plague; this has been recognized and a real fight against this plague is necessary. True, in some of the platforms at the discussion which we have witnessed, this question was raised, at best in a flippant manner, but very often it was examined from a petty-bourgeois point of view.... We must understand that the fight against bureaucracy is an absolutely necessary fight and as complicated as the task of the fight against the petty-bourgeois elements. In our state organization bureaucracy has become a sore to an extent that even our Party program deals with it and that is because bureaucracy is associated with those petty-bourgeois elements and their lack of cohesion. These diseases can be cured only by the unity of the toilers who should not merely welcome the decrees of the Workers' and Peasants' Inspection – have we not enough decrees which are welcomed – but should also exercise their right through the Workers' and Peasants' Inspection, which so far they fail to do not only in the villages, but even in the towns and the capitals! Very often people fail to exercise this right even where the cry against bureaucracy is the loudest. This matter should receive great attention.

V. I. Lenin, *Collected Works,* Russian edition, Vol. XXVI, pp. 219-20.

Take the question of bureaucracy, look at it from the economic aspect. On May 5, 1918, bureaucracy was not in the field of our vision. After six months of the October Revolution, after we had destroyed the old bureaucratic machine root and branch, this evil was not felt by us yet.

Another year passes. At the Eighth Congress of the Russian Communist Party, March 18-23, 1919, a new program is adopted by the Party in which, without fearing to admit the evil, we openly speak about "The partial recrudescence of bureaucracy in the Soviet system," actuated by the desire of disclosing, exposing and pillorying it, the desire of mobilizing the mind, will, and energy for action in the fight against this evil.

Two more years pass. In the spring of 1921, after the Eighth Congress of the Soviets, which (in December 1920) discussed the question of bureaucracy and after the Tenth Congress of the Russian Communist Party (March 1921) which summed up the disputes closely connected with the analysis of bureaucracy, *this* evil rises before us more clearly, more distinctly and more formidably. What are the economic roots of bureaucracy? They are mainly of a two-fold nature: On the one hand a developed bourgeoisie is in need of a bureaucratic machine, in the first place of a military, judicial machine and so forth, precisely directed against the revolutionary movement of the workers (partly also of the peasants). In our case this does not apply. Our courts are class courts against the bourgeoisie. Our army is a class army against the bourgeoisie. There is no bureaucracy in the army but in the institutions serving it. In our country the economic root of bureaucracy is a different one – it is the isolation of the small producer, his poverty, his lack of culture, the absence of roads, illiteracy, the absence of *commodity circulation* between agriculture and industry, the absence of connection and interaction between them.

V. I. Lenin, *Collected Works,* Russian edition, Vol. XXVI, pp. 339-340.

The danger of bureaucracy lies first of all in the fact that it holds back the colossal reserves concealed in the bosom of our social system, not allowing them to be utilized: it tries to nullify the creative initiative of the masses, binds them hand and foot with red tape and aims at reducing every new undertaking of the Party into a petty and insignificant business. The danger of bureaucracy lies, secondly, in the fact that it cannot tolerate having the execution of orders *verified* and strives to transform the principal directions of the leading bodies into a mere sheet of paper divorced from real life. The danger is represented, not only and not so much by the old bureaucratic derelicts in our institutions, as particularly by the new bureaucrats, the Soviet bureaucrats, amongst whom "Communist" bureaucrats play a far from insignificant role. I have in mind those "Communists" who try to replace the creative initiative and independent activity of the millions of the working class and peasantry by office instructions and "decrees," in the virtue of which they believe as a fetish.

The task is to smash bureaucracy in our institutions and organizations, to liquidate bureaucratic "habits" and "customs," and clear the road for the utilization of the reserves of our social order, for the development of the creative initiative and independent activity of the masses.

It is no easy task. It cannot be settled in the twinkling of an eye. But it has to be settled at all costs, if we really want to transform our country on socialist lines.

In its struggle against bureaucracy, the Party works in four directions: in the direction of the development of *self-criticism,* in the direction of *organizing the verification of the execution of orders,* in the direction of *cleansing* the apparatus, and, finally, in the direction of *promoting* to the state apparatus devoted members of the working class from below.

Our task is to concentrate all our forces upon carrying out these measures.

Joseph Stalin, *Leninism,* Vol. П, pp. 312-313.

4. The System of the Dictatorship of the Proletariat and the Role of the Party in It

A. Stalin on the "Mechanism" of the Dictatorship of the Proletariat

I spoke above about the dictatorship of the proletariat from the point of view of its historical inevitability, from the point of view of its class content, from the point of view of its state nature, and, finally, from the point of view of its destructive and creative tasks which are performed throughout an entire historical period described as the period of transition from capitalism to socialism.

Now we must consider the dictatorship of the proletariat from the point of view of its structure, of its "mechanism," of the role and significance of the "belts," the "levers," and the "directing force," the totality of which comprise "the system of the dictatorship of the proletariat" (Lenin), and with the help of which the daily work of the dictatorship of the proletariat is accomplished.

What are these "belts" or "levers" in the system of the dictatorship of the proletariat? What is the "directing force"? Why are they needed?

The levers or the belts are those very mass organizations of the proletariat without whose aid the dictatorship cannot be realized.

The directing force is the advanced detachment of the proletariat, its vanguard, which constitutes the main guiding force of the dictatorship of the proletariat.

The proletariat needs these belts, these levers, and this directing force, because without them it would be, in its struggle for victory, like a weaponless army in face of organized and armed capital. It needs these organizations because without them it would suffer inevitable defeat in its fight for the overthrow of the bourgeoisie, for the consolidation of its own power and for the building of socialism. The systematic help of these organizations and the directing force of the vanguard are indispensable, because without them the dictatorship of the proletariat could not be to any degree durable and firm.

What are these organizations?

First of all there are the workers' *trade unions,* with their national and local ramifications in the shape of a whole series of production, cultural, educational and other organizations. These unite the workers of all trades. They are not Party organizations. The trade unions can be termed the all-embracing organization of the working class which holds power in our country. They constitute a school of Communism. They promote from their midst the best people to carry out leading work in all branches of administration. They form the link between the advanced and the backward elements in the ranks of the working class. They unite the masses of the workers with their vanguard.

Secondly, we have the *soviets* and their numerous central and local ramifications in the shape of administrative, business, military, cultural and other state organizations, together with innumerable voluntary mass organizations of the toilers which group themselves about the first-mentioned organizations and connect them with the general population. The soviets are mass organizations of all the toilers of town and country. They are not Party organizations. The soviets are the direct expression of the dictatorship of the proletariat. All and sundry measures for the strengthening of the dictatorship and for the building of socialism are carried out through the soviets. Through them, the political leadership of the peasantry by the proletariat is realized. The soviets unite the vast toiling masses with the proletarian vanguard.

Thirdly, we have *cooperative* societies of all kinds, with all their ramifications. These are mass organizations of toilers, not Party organizations, in which the toilers are united, primarily as consumers, but also in the course of time as producers (agricultural cooperation). Cooperative societies assume special significance after the consolidation of the dictatorship of the proletariat, during the period of widespread construction. They facilitate the contact between the proletarian vanguard and the peasant masses, and create the possibility of drawing the latter into the channel of socialist construction.

Fourthly, there is the *Young Communist League.* This is a mass organization of the young workers and peasants, is not a Party organization, but it is in close touch with the Party. Its task is to help the Party to educate the younger generation in the spirit of socialism. It provides young reserves for all the other mass organizations of the proletariat in all branches of administration. The Young Communist League acquired special significance after the consolidation of the dictatorship of the proletariat, when widespread cultural and educational work was undertaken by the proletariat.

Lastly, there is the *Party* of the proletariat, its vanguard. The Party's strength lies in the fact that it draws into its ranks all the best elements of the proletariat out of all the mass organizations of the proletariat. Its function is to *combine* the work of all the mass organizations of the proletariat, without exception, and to guide their activities towards a single goal, that of the emancipation of the proletariat. And it is absolutely essential to unite and guide them towards one goal, for otherwise the unity of the struggle of the proletariat and the leadership of the proletarian masses in their fight for power and for the building of socialism is impossible. Only the vanguard of the proletariat, its party, is capable of combining and directing the work of the mass organizations of the proletariat. Only the party of the proletariat, only the party of the Communists, is capable of fulfilling this role of chief leader in the system of the dictatorship of the proletariat.

Why is this?

> ...because, in the first place, it is the common meeting ground of the best elements in the working class that have direct connections with the non-Party organizations of the proletariat and very frequently lead them; because, secondly, the Party, as the meeting ground of the best members of the working class, is the best school for training leaders of the working class, capable of directing every form of organization of their class; because, thirdly, the Party, as the best school for training leaders of the working class, is, by reason of its experience and authority, the only organization capable of centralizing the leadership of the struggle of the proletariat, and in this way of transforming each and every non-Party organization of the working class into an auxiliary body, a transmission belt linking it with the class. (J. Stalin, *Leninism,* Vol. I, p. 94.)

The Party is the main guiding force within the system of the dictatorship of the proletariat. As Lenin puts it, "the Party is the highest form of the class organization of the proletariat."

To sum up: the *trade unions,* as the mass organization of the proletariat, linking the Party with the class primarily in the sphere of production; the *soviets,* as the mass organizations of all toilers, linking the Party with these latter, primarily in the sphere of the state; the *cooperative societies* as mass organizations, mainly of the peasants, linking up the Party with the peasant masses, primarily in the economic field, and serving to draw the peasantry into the work of socialist construction; the *Young Communist League,* as the mass organization of the young workers and peasants, whose mission is to help the proletarian vanguard in the socialist education of the new generation and in training young reserves; and, finally, the Party, as the main directing force within the system of the dictatorship of the proletariat, whose mission it is to lead all these above-mentioned mass organizations – such, in broad outline, is the picture of the "mechanism" of the dictatorship, the picture of the "system of the dictatorship of the proletariat."

Without the Party as the main leading force, a dictatorship of the proletariat at all durable and firm is impossible.

Thus, in the words of Lenin:

> ...on the whole, we have a formally non-Communist, flexible, relatively wide and very powerful proletarian apparatus by means of which the Party is closely linked up with the *class and with the masses,* and by means of which, under the leadership of the Party, the *dictatorship of the class* is realized. (*"Left-Wing" Communism: An Infantile Disorder.*)

Of course, this does not mean that the Party can or should become a substitute for the trade unions, the soviets and the other mass organizations. The Party realizes the dictatorship of the proletariat. It does, so, however, not directly, but with the help of the trade unions, and through the soviets and their ramifications. Without these "belts," anything like a firm dictatorship would be impossible.

> The dictatorship cannot be realized (says Lenin) without several "belts" stretching from the vanguard to the mass of the advanced class, and from this to the mass of the toilers.... The Party, so to speak, absorbs the vanguard of the proletariat, and this vanguard realizes the dictatorship of the proletariat. In the absence of a foundation such as the trade unions, the dictatorship could not be realized, the functions of the state could not be fulfilled. They have to be fulfilled *through* a series of special institutions which are likewise of a new type, namely *through* (My italics. – *J. S.*) the Soviet apparatus. (*Collected Works,* Russian edition, Vol. XXVI, pp. 64-65.)

Joseph Stalin, *Leninism,* Vol. I, pp. 274-78.

B. The Role of the Communist Party under the Dictatorship of the Proletariat.

8. The old "classical" division of the labor movement according to the three forms (party, trade unions, and cooperatives) is obviously out of date. The proletarian revolution in Russia has brought to the front the *soviets* – the main form of the workers' dictatorship. In the near future there will be a new classification everywhere, namely: (1) the Party; (2) the Soviets and (3) the industrial unions. However, the *Party* of the proletariat, *i.e.,* the Communist Party, must

systematically and invariably guide the work in the soviets, as well as the work in the revolutionized industrial unions. The Communist Party, the organized vanguard of the working class, must in an equal measure guide the economic, political and the cultural educational struggle of the working class as a whole. The Communist Party must be the soul of the industrial unions as well as of the soviets of workers' deputies and of all the other proletarian organizations.

The emergence of the soviets as the main historically given form of such dictatorship of the proletariat in no way diminishes the leading role of the Communist Party in the proletarian revolution. The declaration of the German "Left" Communists (see the appeal of their Party of April 14, 1920, addressed to the German proletariat over the signature of "The Communist Labor Party of Germany") to the effect that "the Party too must ever more and more adapt itself to the Soviet idea and assume a proletarian character" – *"dass auch die Partei sich immer mehr dem Rategedanken anpasst und proletarischen Charakter annimmt"* (*Kommunistische Arbeiterzeitung* No. 54), is a confused expression of the idea that the Communist Party must dissolve itself in the Soviets and that the Soviets can replace the Communist Party.

This idea is fundamentally wrong and reactionary. There was a whole period in the history of the Russian Revolution when the Soviets fought against the proletarian party and supported the policy of the agents of the bourgeoisie. The same was to be observed also in Germany, and may happen in other countries too.

On the contrary, in order that the Soviets may achieve their historical mission it is necessary that the Communist Party should be so strong as to be able not merely to "adapt itself" to the soviets but to exercise a *decisive* influence upon their policy, to compel them to give up "adapting themselves" to the bourgeoisie and the White social democracy, and through the Communist fractions in the Soviets to get the latter *to follow* the Communist Party.

Those who propose that the Communist Party should "adapt itself" to the soviets, those who in such an adaptation see the strengthening of the "proletarian character" of the Party, are doing an ill service to the Party as well as to the soviets and understand neither the importance of the Party nor that of the soviets. The stronger the Communist Party created by us in each country the sooner will the "Soviet idea" triumph. The "Soviet idea" is now recognized verbally also by many "independent" socialists and even right socialists. However, only the existence of a strong Communist Party capable of *determining* the policy of the soviets and leading them, will prevent the distortion of the soviet idea by these elements.

9. The Communist Party is necessary to the working class not only *before* the seizure of power and not only *during* the seizure of power but also *after* the power had passed into the hands of the working class. The history of the Russian Communist Party, which has been in power for three years in a huge country, shows that the role of the Communist Party after the seizure of power by the working class, had not only not diminished, but on the contrary has exceedingly increased.

10. On the morrow of the seizure of power by the proletariat, its Party still remains as heretofore only a section of the working class. But it is precisely the section of the working class that organized victory. As we saw in Russia in the course of two decades, and in Germany in the course of a number of years, the Communist Party in the struggle not only against the bourgeoisie but also against those "socialists" who are the conductors of bourgeois influence upon the proletariat has absorbed in its ranks the most staunch, far-sighted and most advanced fighters of the working class. Only provided there is a solid organization of the best section of the working class is it possible to overcome all the difficulties confronting the workers' dictatorship on the morrow of victory. The organization of a new, proletarian Red Army, the actual destruction of the bourgeois state machine and its replacement with the embryo of a new proletarian state apparatus, the fight against the narrow trade aspirations of individual groups of workers, the fight against local and territorial "patriotism," the laying out of new paths in the sphere of creating a new labor discipline – in all these spheres the word of the *party* of the Communists, whose members by their living example lead the majority of the working class, is decisive.

11. The need for the political party of the proletariat disappears only with the complete abolition of classes. It is possible that on the road to this final victory of Communism, the relative importance of the three main proletarian organizations of to-day (the party, the soviets and the industrial unions) will change and that gradually only one type of labor organization will crystallize itself. However, the Communist Party will completely dissolve in the working class only when Communism ceases to be the object of struggle and the

entire working class turns Communist.

"On the Role of the Communist Party in the Proletarian Revolution." *Resolution of the Second Congress of the Communist International.*

C. The Fight Against the Trotskyist Identification of the Dictatorship of the Proletariat with the Dictatorship of the Party

The dictatorship of the proletariat must not be contrasted to the leadership ("dictatorship") of the Party, if correct inter-relationships exist between the Party and the working class, between the vanguard and the working masses. But what follows from this is that it is all the more impermissible to identify the Party with the working class, the leadership ("dictatorship") of the Party with the dictatorship of the working class. *From the circumstance* that the "dictatorship" of the Party must not be set up in contrast to the dictatorship of the proletariat, Comrade Sorin came to the incorrect conclusion that *"the dictatorship of the proletariat is the dictatorship of our Party."* But Lenin speaks not only of the impermissibility of making such a contrast; he also speaks of the impermissibility of contrasting the "dictatorship of the masses" to the "dictatorship of the leaders." *On that basis,* ought we not to identify the dictatorship of the leaders with the dictatorship of the proletariat? If we took that road, we would have to say that the *"dictatorship of the proletariat is the dictatorship of our leaders."* But, properly speaking, it is precisely to this absurdity that the policy of identifying the "dictatorship" of the Party with the dictatorship of the proletariat leads...

Where does Comrade Zinoviev stand on this subject?

Comrade Zinoviev, at bottom, shares Comrade Sorin's point of view of identifying the "dictatorship" of the Party with the dictatorship of the proletariat, with this difference, however, that Comrade Sorin expresses himself more openly and clearly, whereas Comrade Zinoviev "wriggles." It is sufficient to take, say, the following passage in Comrade Zinoviev's book, *Leninism,* to be convinced of this.

What (says Comrade Zinoviev) is the prevailing system in the U.S.S.R. from the standpoint of its class content? It is the dictatorship of the proletariat. What is the direct mainspring of power in the U.S.S.R.? Who gives effect to the power of the working class? The Communist Party! In this sense, we have *the dictatorship of the Party.* (My italics. – *J. S.*) What is the juridical form of power in the U.S.S.R.? What is the new type of state system that was created by the October Revolution? The Soviet system. The one does not in the least contradict the other. (G. Zinoviev, *Leninism,* pp. 370-71.)

That there is no contradiction between the one and the other is, of course, correct, if by dictatorship of the Party in relation to the working class as a whole we mean the leadership of the Party. But how is it possible, *on this basis,* to place a sign of equality between the dictatorship of the proletariat and the "dictatorship" of the Party? Between the Soviet system and the dictatorship of the Party? Lenin identified the Soviet system with the dictatorship of the proletariat, and he was right, for the soviets, *our soviets,* are organizations which rally the toiling masses around the proletariat under the leadership of the Party. But when, where, and in which of his writings, did Lenin place a sign of equality between the "dictatorship" of the Party and the dictatorship of the proletariat, between the "dictatorship" of the Party and the Soviet system, as Comrade Zinoviev does now? Neither the leadership ("dictatorship") of the Party, nor the leadership ("dictatorship") of the leaders contradicts the dictatorship of the proletariat. Ought we not, *on that basis,* proclaim that our country is the country of the dictatorship of the proletariat, *that is to say,* the country of the dictatorship of the Party, *that is to say,* the country of the dictatorship of the leaders? It is precisely to this absurdity that we are led by the "principle" of identifying the "dictatorship" of the Party with the dictatorship of the proletariat that Comrade Zinoviev so stealthily and timidly advocated.

In Lenin's numerous works, I have been able to note only five cases in which he cursorily touches on the question of the dictatorship of the Party.

The first case is in his dispute with the Socialist-Revolutionaries and the Mensheviks, where he states:

When we are reproached with having the dictatorship of one party, and, as you have heard, a proposal is made to establish a united socialist front, we reply: "Yes, the dictatorship of one party! We stand by it, and cannot depart from it, for it is the Party which, in the course of decades, has won the position of vanguard of the whole factory and industrial proletariat." (*Collected Works*, Russian edition, Vol. XXIV, p. 423.)

The second case is in the *Letter to the Workers and Peasants on the Victory over Kolchak.*

> Some people (especially the Mensheviks and the Socialist-Revolutionaries, all, even the "Lefts" among them) are trying to scare the peasants with the bogey of the "dictatorship of one party," the party of Bolsheviks, Communists. The peasants have learned from the case of Kolchak not to be terrified by this bogey. Either the dictatorship (*i.e.,* the iron rule) of the landlords and capitalists, or else the dictatorship of the working class. (*Ibid.,* p. 436.)

The third case is in Lenin's speech at the Second Congress of the Communist International in his controversy with Tanner. I have quoted it above.

The fourth case comprises several lines in *"Left-Wing" Communism: An Infantile Disorder.* The passage in question has already been quoted above.

And the fifth case is in his draft scheme of the dictatorship of the proletariat, published in the *Lenin Miscellany,* Volume III, where there is a sub-heading "Dictatorship of One Party." (See *Lenin Miscellany,* Russian edition, Vol. III, p. 497.)

It should be noted that in two cases out of the five, the second and the fifth, Lenin has the words "dictatorship of one party" in quotation marks, thus clearly emphasizing the inexact, figurative sense of this formula.

It should also be pointed out that in *every one* of these cases when Lenin speaks of the "dictatorship of the Party" *in relation to* the working class, he means not dictatorship in the actual sense of the term ("power based on violence") but the leadership of the Party.

It is characteristic that in *none* of his works, major or secondary, where Lenin discusses or merely alludes to the dictatorship of the proletariat and the function of the Party in the system of the dictatorship of the proletariat, is there any hint whatever that "the dictatorship of the proletariat is the dictatorship of our Party." On the contrary, every page, every line of these works cries out against such a formulation. (See *The State and Revolution, The Proletarian Revolution and Renegade Kautsky, "Left-Wing" Communism: An Infantile Disorder, etc.*)

Even more characteristic is the fact that in the theses of the Second Congress of the Communist International concerning the role of a political party, theses worked out under the direct guidance of Lenin, which he repeatedly referred to in his speeches as a model of the correct formulation of the role and tasks of the Party, we do not find *one word,* literally *not one word,* about the dictatorship of the Party.

What does all this mean?

It means that:

a. Lenin did not regard the formula "the dictatorship of the Party" as being irreproachable and exact, for which reason it is very rarely used in Lenin's works, and is sometimes put in quotation marks.

b. On the few occasions that Lenin was obliged, in controversy with opponents, to speak of the dictatorship of the Party, he usually referred to the "dictatorship of *one party,*" i.e., to the fact that our Party holds power *alone,* that it *does not share* power with *other* parties. Moreover, he always made it clear that the dictatorship of the Party, *in relation to the working class* meant the leadership of the Party, its leading role.

c. In all those cases (and there are thousands) in which Lenin found it necessary to give a scientific definition of the role of the Party in the system of the dictatorship of the proletariat, he spoke *exclusively* of the leading role of the party in relation to the working class.

d. That is why it "never occurred" to Lenin to include the formula "dictatorship of the Party" in the fundamental resolution on the role of the Party (I have in mind the resolution adopted at the Second Congress of the Communist International).

e. Those comrades who identify or try to identify the "dictatorship" of the Party and, consequently, the "dictatorship of the leaders," with the dictatorship of the proletariat are wrong from the point of view of Leninism, and are politically shortsighted, for they thereby violate the conditions of the correct relations between the vanguard and the class.

Needless to say, the formula "dictatorship of the Party," when taken without the above-mentioned qualifications, can create a whole series of perils and political defects in our practical work. When this formula is employed without qualification, it is as though the word is given:

a. *To the non-Party masses:* Don't dare to contradict, don't argue, for the Party can do everything, for we have the dictatorship of the Party.

b. *To the Party cadres:* Act more resolutely; tighten the screw; and there is no need to heed what the non-Party masses say; we have the dictatorship of the Party.

c. *To the Party leaders:* You can enjoy the luxury of a certain amount of self-complacence; you can even give yourselves a few airs, if you like; for we have the dictatorship of the Party, and of course that "means" the dictatorship of the leaders.

It is quite opportune to recall these dangers precisely at the present moment when the political activity of the masses is on the upgrade; when the readiness of the Party to pay close attention to the voice of the masses is of particular value; when sensitiveness to the demands of the masses is a basic precept of our Party; when the Party is called upon to display political caution and particular flexibility in its policy, when the danger of becoming conceited is one of the most serious dangers confronting the Party in its task of correctly leading the masses.

One cannot but recall Lenin's golden words uttered at the Eleventh Congress of our Party:

> Among the masses of the people, we (Communists – *J. S.*) are but drops in the ocean, and we will be able to govern only when we properly express that which the people appreciate. Without this the Communist Party will not lead the proletariat, the proletariat will not take the lead of the masses, and the whole machine will fall to pieces. (V. I. Lenin, *Collected Works,* Russian edition, Vol. XXVII, p. 256.)

"Properly express that which the people appreciate" – this is precisely the necessary condition that insures for the Party the honorable role of the main guiding force in the system of the dictatorship of the proletariat.

Joseph Stalin, *Leninism,* Vol. I, pp. 292-96.

IV. STRENGTHENING TO THE UTMOST THE STATE POWER OF THE PROLETARIAT IN ORDER TO PREPARE THE CONDITIONS FOR THE WITHERING AWAY OF THE STATE

1. Historical Pre-Conditions for the Withering Away of the State

Engels' words regarding the "withering away" of the state are so widely known, they are so often quoted, and they reveal the significance of the customary painting of Marxism to look like opportunism so clearly that we must deal with them in detail. We shall quote the whole passage from which they are taken.

> The proletariat seizes the state power and transforms the means of production in the first instances into State property. But in doing this, it puts an end to itself as the proletariat, it puts an end to all class differences and class antagonisms, it puts an end also to the state as the state. Former society, moving in class antagonisms, has need of the state, that is, an organization of the exploiting class at each period for the maintenance of its external conditions of production; that is, therefore, for the forcible holding down of the exploited class in the conditions of oppression (slavery, villeinage, or serfdom, wage-labor) determined by the existing mode of production. The state was the official representative of society as a whole, its embodiment in a visible corporation; but it was this only in so far as it was the state of that class which itself, in its epoch, represented society as a whole; in ancient times, the state of the slave-owning citizens; in the Middle Ages, of the feudal nobility; in our epoch, of the bourgeoisie. When ultimately it becomes really representative of society as a whole, it makes itself superfluous. As soon as there is no longer any class of society to be held in subjection; as soon as, along with class domination and the struggle for individual existence based on the former anarchy of production, the collisions and excesses arising from these have also been abolished, there is nothing more to be repressed, which would make a special repressive force, a state, necessary. The first act in which the state really comes forward as the representative of soci-

ety as a whole – the taking possession of the means of production in the name of society – is at the same time its last independent act as a state. The interference of the state power in social relations becomes superfluous in one sphere after another, and then ceases of itself. The government of persons is replaced by the administration of things and the direction of the process of production. The state is not "abolished," *it withers away.* It is from this standpoint that we must appraise the phrase "free people's state" – both its justification at times for agitational purposes, and its ultimate scientific inadequacy – and also the demand of the so-called anarchists that the state should be abolished overnight.[*]

It may be said without fear of error that of this argument of Engels', which is so singularly rich in ideas, only one point has become an integral part of socialist thought among modern Socialist Parties, namely, that, according to Marx the state "withers away" – as distinct from the anarchist doctrine of the "abolition of the state." To emasculate Marxism in such a manner is to reduce it to opportunism, for such an "interpretation" only leaves the hazy conception of a slow, even, gradual change, of absence of leaps and storms, of absence of revolution. The current, widespread, mass, if one may say so, conception of the "withering away" of the state undoubtedly means the slurring over, if not the negation, of revolution.

Such an "interpretation" is the crudest distortion of Marxism, advantageous only to the bourgeoisie; in point of theory, it is based on a disregard for the most important circumstances and considerations pointed out, say, in the "summary" of Engels' argument we have just quoted in full.

In the first place, Engels at the very outset of his argument says that, in assuming state power, the proletariat by that "puts an end to the state... as the state." It is not "good form" to ponder over what this means. Generally, it is either ignored altogether, or it is considered to be a piece of "Hegelian weakness" on Engels' part. As a matter of fact, however, these words briefly express the experience of one of the great proletarian revolutions, the Paris Commune of 1871, of which we shall speak in greater detail in its proper place.

---

[*] Frederick Engels, *Herr Eugen Dühring's Revolution in Science (Anti-Dühring),* London and New York, 1935, pp. 314-15. – *Ed.*

As a matter of fact, Engels speaks here of the abolition of the *bourgeois* state by the proletarian revolution, while the words about its withering away refer to the remnants of the *'proletarian* state *after* the Socialist revolution. According to Engels the bourgeois state does not *"wither away,"* but is "put an end to" by the proletariat in the course of the revolution. What withers away after the revolution is the proletarian state or semi-state.

Secondly, the state is a "special repressive force." Engels gives his splendid and extremely profound definition here with complete lucidity. And from it follows that the "special repressive force" for the suppression of the proletariat by the bourgeoisie, for the suppression of the millions of toilers by a handful of the rich, must be superseded by a "special repressive force" for the suppression of the bourgeoisie by the proletariat (the dictatorship of the proletariat). This is precisely what is meant by putting an end to "the state as a state." This is precisely the "act" of taking possession of the means of production in the name of society. And it is obvious that such a substitution of one (proletarian) "special repressive force" for another (bourgeois) "special repressive force" cannot possibly take place in the form of "withering away."

V. I. Lenin, *The State and Revolution,* pp. 22-24.

Marx explains this question most thoroughly in his *Critique of the Gotha Program* (letter to Bracke, May 5, 1875, printed only in 1891 in the *Neue Zeit,* IX-I, and in a special Russian edition). The polemical part of this remarkable work, consisting of a criticism of Lassalleanism, has, so to speak, overshadowed its positive part, namely, the analysis of the connection between the development of Communism and the withering away of the state.

From a superficial comparison of Marx's letter to Bracke (May 5, 1875) with Engels' letter to Bebel (March 28, 1875), which we examined above, it might appear that Marx was much more "pro-state" than Engels, and that the difference of opinion between the two writers on the question of the state was very considerable.

Engels suggested to Bebel that all the chatter about the state be thrown overboard; that the word "state" be eliminated from the program and the word "community" substituted for it. Engels even declared that the Commune was really no longer a state in the proper sense of the word, while Marx spoke of the "future state in Communist society," *i.e.,* apparently he recognized the need for a state even under Communism.

But such a view would be fundamentally wrong. A closer examination shows that Marx's and Engels' views on the state and its withering away were completely identical, and that Marx's expression quoted above refers merely to this *withering away* of the state.

Clearly, there can be no question of defining the exact moment of the *future* withering away – the more so since it must obviously be a rather lengthy process. The apparent difference between Marx and Engels is due to the different subjects they dealt with, the different aims they were pursuing. Engels set out to show Bebel plainly, sharply and in broad outline, the absurdity of the prevailing prejudices concerning the state, shared to no small degree by Lassalle. Marx, on the other hand, only touched upon *this* question in passing, being interested mainly in another subject, *viz.,* the *development* of Communist society.

The whole theory of Marx is an application of the theory of development – in its most consistent, complete, thought out and replete form – to modern capitalism. It was natural for Marx to raise the question of applying this theory both to the forthcoming collapse of capitalism and to the *future* development of *future* Communism.

On the basis of what *data* can the question of the future development of future Communism be raised?

On the basis of the fact that *it has its origin* in capitalism, that it develops historically from capitalism, that it is the result of the action of a social force to which capitalism *has given birth.* There is no trace of an attempt on Marx's part to conjure up a Utopia, to make idle guesses about what cannot be known. Marx treats the question of Communism in the same way as a naturalist would treat the question of the development of, say, a new biological species, if he knew that such and such was its origin, and such and such the direction in which it was changing.

Marx, first of all, brushes aside the confusion the Gotha Program brings into the question of the relation between state and society. He writes:

> "Present-day society" is the capitalist society which exists in all civilized countries, more or less free from mediaeval admixture, more or less modified by the special historical development of each country and more or less developed. On the other hand the "present-day state" changes

with a country's frontier. It is different in the Prusso-German Empire from what it is in Switzerland, it is different in England from what it is in the United States. The "present-day state" is therefore a fiction.

Nevertheless, the different states of the different civilized countries, in spite of their varied diversity of form, all have this in common, that they are based on modern bourgeois society, only one more or less capitalistically developed. They have therefore also certain essential features in common. In this sense, it is possible to speak of the "present-day state" in contrast with the future, in which its present root, bourgeois society, will have died away.

The question then arises: what transformation will the states undergo in communist society? In other words, what social functions will remain in existence that are analogous to the present functions of the state? This question can only be answered scientifically and one does not get a flea-hop nearer to the problem by a thousand-fold combination of the word people with the word state.

Having thus ridiculed all talk about a "people's state," Marx formulates the question and warns us, as it were, that to arrive at a scientific answer one must rely only on firmly established scientific data.

The first fact that has been established with complete exactitude by the whole theory of development, by science as a whole – a fact which the Utopians forgot, and which is forgotten by present-day opportunists who are afraid of the Socialist revolution – is that, historically, there must undoubtedly be a special stage or epoch of *transition* from capitalism to Communism.

V. I. Lenin, *The State and Revolution,* pp. 69-71.

2. Conditions for the Withering Away of the State

The state withers away in so far as there are no longer any capitalists, any classes, and, consequently, no *class* can be suppressed.

But the state has not yet completely withered away, since there still remains the protection of "bourgeois right" which sanctified actual inequality. For the complete withering away of the state, complete Communism is necessary.

(V. I. Lenin, *The State and Revolution,* p. 78.)

The more complete the democracy becomes, the nearer the moment approaches, when it becomes unnecessary. The more democratic the "state" of the armed workers – which is "no longer a state in the proper sense of the word" – becomes, the more rapidly does *the state* begin to wither away. (*Ibid.,* p. 84.)

Communism alone is capable of giving a really complete democracy and the more complete it is the more quickly will it become unnecessary and wither away of itself. (*Ibid.*)

We are in favor of the state's withering away and at the same time we stand for the strengthening of the dictatorship of the proletariat, which represents the most powerful and mighty authority of all forms of state which have existed up to the present day. The highest possible development of the power of the state, with the object of preparing the conditions *for* the dying out of the state: that is the Marxist formula. Is, it "contradictory"? Yes, it is "contradictory." But this contradiction is a living thing, and completely reflects Marxist dialectics.

Joseph Stalin, *Leninism,* Vol. II.

Certain comrades interpreted the thesis on the abolition of classes, the establishment of classless society and the dying out of the state, to mean justification of laziness and complacency, justification of the counter-revolutionary theory of the subsiding of the class struggle and the weakening of state authority. Needless to say, such people cannot have anything in common with our Party. These are either degenerates, or double dealers, who must be driven out of the Party. The abolition of classes is not achieved by subduing the class struggle, but by intensifying it. The state will die out not by the weakening of state authority, but by strengthening it to the utmost necessary for the purpose of finally crushing the remnants of the dying classes and for organizing defense against the capitalist environment, which is far from being destroyed as yet, and will not soon be destroyed.

Joseph Stalin, *Report at the Joint Plenum of the Central Committee and the Central Control Commission of the Communist Party of the Soviet Union,* January 1933, pp. 54-55.

3. The Fight for the Strengthening of the Soviet State and the Tightening of Socialist Discipline During the First Period of Socialist Construction

...Dictatorship is a big word, and big words should not be scattered to the winds. Dictatorship means an iron rule, revolutionarily bold, quick and ruthless in suppressing exploiters as well as hooligans. But our government is too soft, very often it is more like jelly than iron. We must not forget for a moment that the bourgeois and petty-bourgeois surroundings are militating against the Soviet government in two ways: On the one hand they are operating from outside, by the methods of the Savinkovs, Gotzes, Gegechkoris and Kornilovs, through conspiracies and rebellions, and through their filthy "ideological" mirror, through the flood of lies and slander in the Cadet, Right Socialist-Revolutionary and Menshevik press; on the other hand, these elements operate from within and take advantage of every element of disintegration, of every weakness, in order to bribe, to increase indiscipline, laxity and chaos. The nearer we approach the complete military suppression of the bourgeoisie, the more dangerous the elements of petty-bourgeois anarchy become. And the fight against these elements cannot be waged solely with the aid of propaganda and agitation, solely by organizing competition and by selecting organizers. The struggle must also be waged by means of coercion.

In proportion as the fundamental task of the government becomes, not military suppression, but administration, the typical manifestation of suppression and coercion will not be shooting on the spot, but trial by court. In this respect after November 7 (October 25), 1917, the revolutionary masses took the right course and demonstrated the virility of the revolution by setting up their own workers' and peasants' courts, even before the decrees dissolving the bourgeois bureaucratic legal apparatus were passed. But our revolutionary people's courts are extremely, incredibly weak. One feels that we have not yet changed the attitude of the people towards the courts as towards something official and alien, an attitude which is the effect of the yoke of the landlords and the bourgeoisie. It is not yet sufficiently realized that the court is an organ which enlists all the poor in the work of state administration (for the work of the courts is one of the functions of state administration), that the court is *an organ* of the government of the proletariat and of the poor peasants, that the court is an instrument for *inculcating discipline.*

There is not yet sufficient appreciation of the simple and obvious fact that the principal misfortunes of Russia at the present time, hunger and unemployment, cannot be remedied by enthusiasm but only by extensive, all-embracing, nation-wide organization and discipline in order to increase, deliver and distribute in proper time the output of bread for the people and bread for industry (fuel), neither is it fully understood that those who violate labor discipline in any factory or enterprise, are *responsible* for starvation and unemployment, and that we must find those who are guilty, put them to trial and ruthlessly punish them. The petty-bourgeois influences against which we must now wage a persistent struggle manifest themselves precisely in the failure to appreciate the national economic and political connections between starvation and unemployment and general laxity in matters of organization and discipline, in the tenacity of the *petty-bourgeois maxim:* Grab as much as you can, and hang the consequences.

V. I. Lenin, *Collected Works,* Russian edition, Vol. XXII, pp. 459-60.

...During the transition from capitalism to socialism the Dictatorship of the Proletariat is an absolute necessity; this truth has been fully confirmed also in the practice of our Revolution. However, the dictatorship presupposes a really revolutionary power which firmly and ruthlessly suppresses both the exploiters and the hooligans; but our government is too soft. Obedience, and unconditional obedience, during work (as demanded for instance by the Railway decree) to the orders issued by the soviet leaders, dictators, who are elected or appointed by the soviet institutions and endowed with dictatorial power, is very inadequately enforced. It is the effect of the petty-bourgeois influence, of small proprietory habits, strivings and moods which are in utter contradiction to proletarian discipline and socialism. All class-conscious proletarians must devote their attention to the fight against these petty-bourgeois elements.

Ibid., p. 501.

4. The Fight for the Strengthening of the Proletarian Dictatorship at the Present Stage

The basis of our system is public property, just as private property is the basis of capitalism. The capitalists proclaimed private property to be sacred and inviolable when they, in their time, were striking to consolidate the capitalist system. All the more reason therefore why the Communist should proclaim public property to be sacred and inviolable in order, by that, to consolidate the new socialist forms of economy in all spheres of production and trade. To permit pilfering and theft of public property – no matter whether it is state property or the property of cooperative societies and collective farms – and to ignore such counter-revolutionary outrages, is tantamount to aiding and abetting the undermining of the Soviet system, which rests on the base of public property. These were the reasons that prompted our Soviet government to pass the recent law for the protection of public property. That law is the basis of revolutionary law at the present time. And it is the primary duty of every Communist, of every worker, and of every collective farmer, to strictly carry out this law.

It is said that revolutionary law at the present time does not differ in any way from revolutionary law in the first period of N.E.P., that revolutionary law at the present time is a reversion to revolutionary law of N.E.P. This is absolutely wrong. The edge of revolutionary law in the first period of N.E.P. was turned mainly against the extremes of War Communism, against "illegal" confiscation and imposition of taxes. It guaranteed the security of the property of the private owner, of the capitalist, provided he strictly observed the laws of the Soviets. The position in regard to revolutionary law at the present time is entirely different. The edge of revolutionary law at the present time is turned against thieves and wreckers of social economy, against hooligans and the plunderers of public property. However, the main concern of revolutionary law at the present time is the protection of public property and of no other.

That is why to wage the fight to protect public property, a fight waged by *all* the measures and by all the means placed at our command by the laws of the Soviet Government, is one of the fundamental tasks of the Party.

A strong and powerful dictatorship of the proletariat – that is what we must have now in order to shatter the last remnants of the dying classes and to frustrate their thieving designs.

Joseph Stalin, *Report at the Joint Plenum of the Central Committee and Central Control Commission of the Communist Party of the Soviet Union,* January, 1933, pp. 53-54.

Take for example the question of building *classless socialist society*. The Seventeenth Party Conference declared that we are marching towards classless socialist society. It goes without saying that classless society cannot come by itself. It has to be won and built by the efforts of all the toilers, by strengthening the organs of the dictatorship of the proletariat, by extending the class struggle, by abolishing classes, by liquidating the remnants of the capitalist classes in battles with the enemy, both internal and external.

The thing is. clear, one would think.

And yet, who does not know that the promulgation of this clear and elementary thesis of Leninism has given rise to not a little confusion and unhealthy moods among a certain section of Party members? The thesis – advanced as a slogan – about our advancing towards classless society is interpreted by them as a spontaneous process. And they begin to reason in the following way: If it is a classless society, then we can relax the class struggle, we can relax the dictatorship of the proletariat and generally abolish the state, which in any case has got to die out soon. And they dropped into a state of moon-calf ecstasy in the expectation that soon there will be no classes and therefore no class struggle, and therefore no cares and worries, and therefore it is possible to lay down our arms and retire – to sleep and to wait for the advent of classless society.

There can be no doubt that this confusion of mind and these moods are as like as two peas to the well-known views of the Right deviationists who believed that the old must automatically grow into the new, and that one fine day we shall wake up and find ourselves in socialist society.

As you see, the remnants of the ideology of the defeated anti-Leninist groups can be revived, and have not lost their tenacity by a long way.

It goes without saying that if this confusion of mind and these non-Bolshevik moods overcame the majority of our Party, the Party would find itself demobilized and disarmed.

Joseph Stalin, "Report to the Seventeenth Congress of the C.P.S.U.," *Socialism Victorious,* pp. 64-65.

Despite the desperate resistance of the class enemies and the attacks upon the Party by the agents of the class enemies – the opportunists of all shades – the policy of the Party, the policy of its C.C., has triumphed. It has triumphed, first, because this policy corresponds to the class interests of the millions of workers and peasants, and, second, because the Bolshevik Party, its C.C., not only proclaimed political slogans but were able in a Bolshevik manner to organize the masses to put these slogans into practice, to organize and rearrange every organ and apparatus of the proletarian dictatorship in keeping with the new tasks of the reconstruction period.

At the Sixteenth Party Congress, Comrade Stalin, in characterizing the essence of the Bolshevik offensive in the period of reconstruction, pointed to the necessity of

> ...organizing the reconstruction of all the practical work of our trade union, co-operative, Soviet and all other kinds of mass organizations in keeping with the demands of the reconstruction period; in organizing in them a nucleus of the most active and revolutionary workers, pushing aside and isolating the opportunists, narrow craft unionists and bureaucratic elements; driving out of them the hostile and degenerate elements, promoting new workers from below... *mobilizing* the Party itself to organize the whole offensive; strengthening and pulling together the Party organizations.

Guiding itself by these precepts, the Party during the period under review carried out important measures to improve the work of the Soviet, economic and Party organizations, to rearrange their work in keeping with the demands of the successful fulfillment of the decisions and slogans of the Party and the government.

The most weighty of these measures were:

1. The further development of districting – the abolition of *okrugs** the creation of new districts and the organization of the political departments of the machine and tractor stations and Soviet farms which have brought the leadership closer to the village, to the collective farm, and which have corrected the major shortcomings in the work in the countryside; the organization of regions in the Ukraine; the splitting up of several regions (*oblasts and krais†*) and the like.

2. The splitting up of the People's Commissariats, of the chief boards and trusts, thus bringing the leadership nearer to the lower production links, to the factories; the subdivision of the Supreme Council of National Economy into three People's Commissariats –

---

* Former territorial unit embracing several districts. – *Ed.*

† Larger territorial units each embracing several *okrugs*. – *Ed.*

the People's Commissariat of Heavy Industry, the People's Commissariat of Light Industry, the People's Commissariat of Timber; of the People's Commissariat of Agriculture into two People's Commissariats – the People's Commissariat of Agriculture and the People's Commissariat of Soviet Farms; of the People's Commissariat of Trade into two People's Commissariats – the People's Commissariat of Supply and the People's Commissariat of Foreign Trade; of the People's Commissariat of Ways of Communication into two People's Commissariats and one board – the People's Commissariat of Ways of Communication, the People's Commissariat of Waterways and the Central Board of Road Transport, and so forth.

3. The carrying through of the purging of the Soviet and economic organs and the curtailment of their personnel; the abolition of the functional system in the coal industry and railway transport for the purpose of fighting red tape, bureaucratic methods of leadership and depersonalization, the shifting of the best engineers and technicians from the apparatus and the office directly to production.

4. The splitting up of the trade unions which has led to the strengthening of the role of the C.C.'s of the industrial trade unions; the reorganization of the system of supply – the organization of workers' supply departments attached to the factory managements with an extension of their right and the organization of the Workers' Closed Cooperative Stores.

5. The organization of political departments in railway and airway transport, the institution of the system of Party organizers in the coal industry and other industrial branches including the People's Commissariat of Waterways.

6. The carrying out of the purging of the Party as the highest form of Party self-criticism and the consolidation of the Party as the organized vanguard of socialist construction.

The success of this work was insured by the development of self-criticism and the mobilization of the activity of the masses for creative construction, by socialist competition and shock brigade work.

The prompt raising and carrying out into life by the Party of all these organizational questions insured the Party and socialist construction against a discrepancy between the correct line of the Party and the organizational work required to carry out this line.

The Seventeenth Congress of the C.P.S.U. holds that despite the successes achieved in carrying out the rearrangement of the levers of the proletarian dictatorship, the organizational and practical work nevertheless lags behind the demands of the political directives and does not satisfy the requirements of the present period – the period of the Second Five-Year Plan – which have grown immensely.

The present period of socialist construction is characterized by the still greater complexity of the tasks, by the still higher level of the demands presented to the leadership. The principal tasks of the Second Five-Year Plan period – the final liquidation of the capitalist elements, the overcoming of the survivals of capitalism in the economy and consciousness of people, the completion of the reconstruction of the whole of national economy on the basis of modern technique, the mastery of the new technique and the new enterprises, the mechanization of agriculture and the raising of its productivity – urgently put the question of raising the quality of work in all branches of industry, first and foremost the quality of organizational and practical leadership.

Now that the general line of the Party has conquered, now that the policy of the Party has been tested by life, by the experience not only of the members of the Party but also of millions of workers and toiling peasants, the task of raising organizational work to the level of political leadership rises in all its scope. The organizational problem, while remaining a problem subordinate to problems of policy, nevertheless in view of this acquires *exceptional* significance for the further successes of socialist construction.

"Resolution on the report of L. M. Kaganovich at the XVII Congress of the C.P.S.U.," *Socialism Victorious,* pp. 673-76.